53 interesting ways to assess your students

Edited by Victoria Burns

P&H

ISBN: 978-1-907076-54-1 (ePub edition)
978-1-907076-53-4 (PDF edition)
978-1-907076-52-7 (paperback edition)

Published under The Professional and Higher Partnership imprint by Frontinus Ltd
Registered office: Suite 7, Lyndon House, 8 King's Court, Willie Snaith Road, Newmarket, Suffolk, CB8 7SG, UK

Company website: http://pandhp.com

Third edition, published 2015.

Based on an earlier edition by Graham Gibbs, Sue Habeshaw and Trevor Habeshaw, published by Technical and Educational Services Ltd (first published 1986). Revised and updated for this edition by Victoria Burns.

Credits
Abstract: Anthony Haynes
Copy-editing: Karen Haynes
Cover image: Rika Newcombe (www.rikanewcombe.co.uk)
Cover design and typesetting: Benn Linfield (www.bennlinfield.com)
Proofreading: Will Dady
Printers: Berforts (www.berforts.co.uk) and Lightning Source (www.lightningsource.com)

Disclaimer

The material contained in this publication is provided in good faith as general guidance. The advice and strategies contained herein may not be suitable for every situation. No liability can be accepted by Frontinus Ltd for any liability, loss, risk, or damage which is incurred as a consequence, whether direct or indirect, of using or applying any of the contents of this book or the advice or guidance contained therein.

The publisher and the author make no warranties or representations with respect to the completeness or accuracy of the contents of this work and specifically disclaim all warranties, including without limitation warranties of fitness for a particular purpose. No warranty may be created or extended by sales or promotional materials.

Professional and Higher Education: series information

Titles in the Professional and Higher Education series include:

53 interesting things to do in your lectures
53 interesting things to do in your seminars and tutorials
53 interesting ways of helping your students to study
53 ways to deal with large classes
53 interesting ways to communicate your research
53 interesting ways to assess your students

Contents

Abstract

53 ways of assessing students are presented. The themes covered include: written assessment tasks in various genres; examinations; problem-based activities (such as design tasks) and authentic forms of assessment (such as publishing online); assessment through events (such as presentations) and over longer periods of time (for example, via a portfolio); and interpersonal aspects, such as group work, student involvement, and feedback. Overall, the text provides reflective practitioners in professional and higher education with practical ways to develop broad, flexible assessment repertoires.

Key terms: authentic assessment; assessment; examinations; feedback; learning; marking; peer assessment; practicals; presentations; quality; self-assessment; tasks; and written assessment.

Publishers' foreword

The original edition of 53 *interesting ways to assess your students* was published in a series called 'Interesting ways to teach'. It was written by Graham Gibbs, Sue Habeshaw and Trevor Habeshaw – all of them experienced teachers – and published by their company, Technical and Educational Services. A few years ago, we were very pleased to acquire from them the rights to this and other titles from their popular series. 53 *interesting ways to assess your students* is the fifth such title that we have republished.

Although much of the text of this new edition is based on that of the first, it has been thoroughly reviewed and updated by the new volume editor, Vikki Burns, and her team of contributors. As well as revising material from the original edition, they have introduced or expanded themes such as authentic assessment, quality assurance, equal opportunities and academic misconduct. Vikki's team, credited at the end of individual items, comprise Gavin Brown (items 17, 44 and 47); Robin Burrow (2 and 3); Kate Edwards (4, 6, 7 and 20); and Karl Nightingale (10, 11, 14 and 39). The new items contributed by Vikki herself are 1, 5, 9, 12, 15, 18–19, 20–24, 27–28, 38, 42–43, 46, 48–49, and 51–53.

Anthony Haynes & Karen Haynes

Editor's preface

Like its predecessor, this book is an accessible introduction to a range of assessment strategies. Although our suggestions draw on educational theories and empirical evidence, this is not our focus; instead, we provide simple descriptions of a variety of approaches, along with brief rationales and practical advice for their use.

If you are new to assessment, the book will clarify the (usually unwritten) considerations, and help you make informed choices about the first tasks you set. More experienced staff will find a wealth of ideas to adapt and extend their practice, along with information to help justify and implement their choices. If you are responsible for whole academic programmes, the book will help you design an effective, varied, and progressive portfolio of tasks. It would also be a useful aid for staff training or collaborative discussions. As university lecturers ourselves, the book is based on our experiences and knowledge of higher education, but teachers or trainers in other settings will also find suggestions to adapt for their own contexts.

We would recommend that all readers start with item 1: Choosing assessment methods, and then dip in and out of the rest as preferred. If you are interested in exploring further, or are studying for a teaching and learning qualification, this book will be a useful starting point before a more in-depth review of the literature surrounding your chosen assessment method. Whatever your experience and goals, we hope that you find reading the book as useful and enjoyable as we found writing it.

Vikki Burns

Contributors

Dr Victoria Burns, School of Sport, Exercise, and Rehabilitation Sciences, University of Birmingham, UK (volume editor) with:

- Dr Gavin Brown, School of Computer Science, University of Manchester, UK
- Dr Robin Burrow, Business School, The University of Buckingham, UK
- Dr Kate Edwards, Faculty of Health Sciences, The University of Sydney, Australia
- Dr Karl Nightingale, School of Immunity and Infection, College of Medical and Dental Sciences, University of Birmingham, UK

Introduction

1 Choosing assessment methods

Assessment is at the heart of the learning experience. Students put more time and effort into assessment tasks than any other aspect of their learning, and considerable amounts of staff time are spent supporting and marking assessments. The choice of assessment tasks affects the motivation of students, what they spend time doing, what they perceive as important, and indeed their very conceptualisation of what learning is. It is unfortunate, therefore, that the choice of assessment method is often a relative after-thought, usually determined once the curriculum content has been devised. This choice is likely to be based largely on historical precedents, from a limited range of options, and other practicalities such as student numbers and/or staff time. Instead, staff should be encouraged to first consider *why* the students are being assessed and what it is hoped that they will learn. These fundamental principles then underpin the choice of *how* and *when* to assess the students to best support these outcomes.

Why assess?

For many members of staff, the purpose of assessment is to judge how much a student has learned, what they are now able to do, and how they compare to the rest of the cohort. In this sense, it is an assessment *of* learning, focussing primarily on measurement of student attainment. In contrast, assessment *for* learning prioritises how the assessment task can guide student behaviour and promote more effective learning. For example, if you want students to understand research design, you could ask them to design a research project. If you want students to be able to apply knowledge in a clinical or employment setting, you could ask students to critically review and comment on videos of practice. If you want students to work effectively in groups, you could assess the group process by portfolio and peer assessment, for example, as well as the end product. In this way, the assessment task explicitly requires students to engage in desirable learning behaviours – it doesn't just measure their declarative knowledge.

Similarly, staff must consider the purpose of the work when deciding whether to make the task formative or summative. In formative assessment, the mark achieved does not contribute to the final grade. The priority instead is to give an opportunity for students to practise and get feedback on their work to improve future performance. This may be particularly appropriate at the early stages of a module or course. Summative assessments, which contribute to the final grade, can be set at any stage, but are more common later in the module or course. Here, assessment of learning is clearly an important component of the assessment. However, this does not mean that summative assessments cannot focus on assessment for learning and improve future performance. On the contrary, as students typically engage more with summative assessment, they can be an important opportunity to guide learning in a meaningful way.

How and when to assess

There is a huge range of assessment tasks available to teaching staff in higher education, but we often stay within the traditional boundaries of essays, presentations, and unseen exams. The tasks covered in this book illustrate the range available and discuss the benefits and considerations of each. There are always constraints, depending on the number of students and the time pressure on the staff, but many of these tasks are no more onerous than their traditional alternatives. For some professional courses, the accrediting bodies may restrict the methods of assessment (perhaps as a safeguard against cheating). However, it is often possible to gain permission to introduce a mixed assessment diet as long as the methods align with the learning outcomes and the quality assurance processes are clear.

Hand in hand with choice of assessment task are decisions about the weightings and timings of different pieces of work. These allow staff to make implicit statements about emphasis and balance. For example, it is common for final year work to be more heavily weighted than mid-degree work, to reflect the further learning that has occurred at this point. You can also take this approach within a module, where early work has a smaller weighting than later work. This encourages students to engage early but without the pressure of a large assessment early on. If the task is chosen carefully, then it can also encourage useful preparatory behaviour. For example, if you want students to start engaging with recent publications rather than relying on textbooks, set them an early assessment that requires them to choose, and review or present, a publication from within the last year. They will then have to screen many options in order to choose an appropriate article, and in doing so, will read far more widely than they would have done given the general encouragement to keep up to date with current literature. This approach is particularly valuable where the later work builds on this early work, and enables the students to apply their feedback to improve their work. Manipulating weightings can also be useful if you may want to include an exam as a safeguard against cheating but feel reluctant to devote very many marks to it. In this case you could give it a relatively small weighting (e.g. 10 per cent) but make passing the exam a progression requirement. Finally, applying a smaller weighting can also be a useful way to introduce more innovative or unusual assessments, without the students feeling it is too 'risky'.

Chapter 1
Essays

2 Standard essay

A 'standard' essay is essentially a piece of writing on a particular topic and is one of the most popular forms of assessment. There are good reasons for this popularity. Essays can be a useful way of assessing students' *deep* learning – students' knowledge and understanding of a topic area. They also evaluate whether students can communicate a clear and coherent written argument that pulls together relevant evidence to address a particular question.

There is a real art to writing good essay questions for students. At their core, all essay questions should enable students to articulate their knowledge and understanding of a particular topic area. In addition to this, they should also give students the opportunity to present their own analysis and synthesis. Essays are not usually just about whether students can describe what they know about something, but about whether they integrate this knowledge and synthesise their own individualised argument. Within the boundaries of a specific topic area, essays give students the opportunity to put forward their own voice.

What follows are some examples* of possible essay structures, together with some notes about their use:

Write an essay on...

Q. Write an essay on fluid mechanics.

Q. Select one topic that is of contemporary interest in African education. Outline a brief background of the topic, and discuss the key issues of current concern.

These open-ended questions give students the freedom to set the scope of their own essay and to structure the work themselves. This may allow excellent students to shine, but many students may be overwhelmed by the scope offered to them, and may struggle to select material and present it effectively. The expectations of the marker, in terms of what constitutes a good answer, remain opaque. Further, if used in exams, students can revise and prepare complete answers on likely topics, and trot them out without thought or understanding. Even without this sort of preparation, such questions may enable students to cobble together enough disconnected facts and ideas to pass without revealing much insight.

Describe, Give an account of, Compare, Contrast, Explain

Q. Describe the six key features of episodic analgesia. Can episodic analgesia help us to understand the specificity theory of pain?

Q. Outline how the classical Hollywood hero was undermined or challenged in the 1960s post-classical period by reference to at least two films from the course.

These questions set a clear scope for the essay, including some quantification of the number of examples expected. This can help the student to structure an appropriate answer. However, by using 'describe' or 'outline', these questions do not explicitly require the student to express a viewpoint or conclusion. They may be more appropriate, therefore, at lower levels of study. If, however, there is such a requirement, it should be clearly stated either in the instructions, or as an additional 'sub' question, as in the first example.

Simple questions

Q. How far is poverty just another name for inequality?

Q. Is language necessary for theory of mind and is theory of mind necessary for language?

As with 'describe' questions, simple questions set the scope of an essay, but often provide less guidance on the marker's expectations. They are useful for discriminating between students' level of understanding. However, the instructions benefit from providing specific guidance about the level of examples or evidence expected in the answers to such questions.

Assess, Analyse, Evaluate

Q. Critically discuss the link between corporate social responsibility and corporate performance.

Q. Analyse, with examples, the key steps in assessing earthquake risk.

These questions require not just information from the student, but also explicitly request critical analysis and a reasoned conclusion. This makes these some of the most appropriate stems for essay questions, particularly at higher levels.

Quotation: Discuss (or Comment, or Query)

Q. Jeremy Bentham famously described natural rights as 'Nonsense on stilts'. Outline the utilitarian critique of rights and discuss its validity.
Q. 'Oxidative stress causes immune aging.' Discuss.

Using a quotation as a stimulus can encourage students to challenge expert opinion, and present their own analyses. However, if its purpose is mainly decorative, then students may have problems working out what is important about the quotation. This format also provides less information about what is required in the answer; this can be addressed effectively by pairing a quotation with a more focussed question, as in the first example here.

Trick or obscure questions

Q. Can I be mistaken about my own level of wellbeing?
Q. How fat was Falstaff? Do Shakespeare's plays present the bodies of his characters in a consistent fashion?

These questions capture the imagination and provide an opportunity for innovative thinking. However, there is a danger that they are only fully understood by the people who set them and their favourite students. It is important to ensure that students have a good understanding of how to interpret such questions and to link them to their learning materials. Again, this can be aided by adding a 'sub' section to support the more oblique question, as in the second example.

Robin Burrow

*Questions in this chapter are based on real examples from the archives of the University of Birmingham, UK (copyright: University of Birmingham).

3 Structured essay

Structured essays are slightly different from other forms of essay-based assessment (see **2** and **4**), because they specify the key elements of the content in advance. This type of assessment is particularly useful if you want to assess some specific aspect of students' learning, or if you need an efficient marking process, as structured essays tend to be shorter. However, one of the potential limitations of this type of assessment is that it is sometimes difficult to tell whether students are able to judge for themselves which things are important, without prompting. Ultimately, you have to decide what it is that you want to assess. Do you want to assess specific knowledge, or the student's ability to identify what is important?

There are a variety of ways to set structured essays, but the three main ones are: (1) full essays which provide a road map that helps to guide students' answers; (2) note-form essays, which are a more extreme version of this, in which only short answers are required; (3) annotated bibliographies which can assess student understanding of a particular area of research literature.

Full structured essays

These essay questions guide students through the required sections, but still require the students to produce extended pieces of writing. This still allows an assessment of higher level understanding, but reduces the opportunity for independent approaches to answering the question. For example*:

Q. Is *Heart of Darkness* a Victorian novel? Discuss the characteristic features of Victorian novels. Identify the key differences between Victorian and post-Victorian novels. Highlight the main characteristics of *Heart of Darkness*. On the basis of the preceding three sections, draw conclusions about the extent to which *Heart of Darkness* is a Victorian novel.

Q. Identify and discuss some of the determinants of urban land values and their impact on urban development. In your answer you should:

a Define the following terms:
- property rights in land
- zoning
- site value rating;

b Explain the influence of these terms in determining land values;

c Select one activity of public authorities, and one market factor, which affect land values and explain how each might influence urban development.

Note-form essay

Note-form essays are a more extreme version of the full structured essay. This type of question is used most often to assess the recall of key items of information or test simple understanding of terms, formulae, apparatus, tools and so on. It is less suitable for assessing analysis, synthesis of ideas, or creativity. Sometimes note-form questions are used to assess whether students understand what is significant about a topic. For example:

Q. List the main economic factors which affect the pattern of changing land values. For each factor, itemise its limitations and potentialities for predicting future urban development. Your answer may be in note form.

Q. Briefly describe the significance for oil exploration of each of the following microfossil types: [etc.].

Note-form essays are easier and quicker (though less interesting) to mark, but they do have a number of disadvantages. Students who have plenty to say about the topics and are obliged to select the main points are faced with the problem of guessing which aspects the marker thinks are most important. Conversely, poor students can gain marks by writing down whatever comes into their heads about any of the topics, without having to illustrate understanding. They are also less effective for assessing more nuanced understanding of particular points.

Annotated bibliographies

An annotated bibliography requires the students to conduct a literature search in a particular topic, select an appropriate list of the most pertinent papers, and provide a short commentary on each source. This commentary should go beyond a mere description of the main findings of each paper, to include some critical notes about each source. To do this effectively, the student must be able to select the most important papers on a topic, and identify their key contributions and limitations. This can be used as an effective assessment in its own right, or as the first stage in a more extensive piece of work, such as a dissertation.

Robin Burrow

*Questions in this chapter are based on real examples from the archives of the University of Birmingham, UK (copyright: University of Birmingham).

4 Literature review

A literature review provides an overview of a field of work, exploring what has already been said and shown, what lines of inquiry have been followed, hypotheses made and methods used. Critical analysis allows the identification of gaps in current understanding and potential directions of future work, while also establishing the broader relevance of the area. For students, writing a literature review incorporates many skills necessary for deep learning, such as critical evaluation and analysis. It can be used as a 'standalone' piece of assessment, to assess understanding of an area of research; or as an early task in, for example, a project module, in which students need to understand the background literature before conducting their own research.

Assessment design considerations

The primary objective of the review must be clear. It could focus on a theory, a methodological approach, current research findings, and so on. The scope will vary according to level of the student; a relatively narrow focus and small body of literature will be more typical at lower undergraduate levels, developing to larger bodies of literature for dissertations and theses.

Literature reviews can be either narrative or systematic. A systematic review follows explicit guidelines for the search, inclusion and appraisal of pieces, while a narrative review is more subjective and informal in its methods. Although systematic reviews are more common in clinical and preclinical subjects, their well-defined guidelines (for example, Preferred Reporting items for Systematic Reviews and Meta-Analyses or PRISMA) can help students to structure their searches in any area of research. Regardless of the type of review, students will need support to be successful and are likely to benefit from regular feedback. Before setting a literature review, it can be useful to include shorter assignments, in which students summarise and critique single studies, or a small set of studies.

Students are often unsure how many references they are expected to use in a literature review. Although this can vary depending on the subject, setting an approximate guideline is beneficial. It encourages students who were only reading a limited range of studies, while also encouraging other students to select the most relevant or best examples rather than simply giving an encyclopaedic list. Discussing citations for the literature review also provides an opportunity to discuss good academic practice and the avoidance of plagiarism (see item **52**).

Criteria and rubric

Clear assessment criteria, including length and plagiarism guidelines, along with marking rubrics should be developed to guide students and assessors. An example rubric is below. It makes the requirements more explicit, and therefore helps the student to structure and write their work. It is helpful to familiarise students with these rubrics through formative peer assessment (see item **39**).

	Low/Poor	**Medium/Good**	**High/Excellent**
Aim and Background	Provides some background information and attempts to set the scene. Key ambiguities undefined. Aims of the review are stated, although not clearly.	Provides detailed background information. Area mostly covered and sets the scene well. Specific aims of the review are stated.	Comprehensive and detailed background. Weaves a clear and logical argument, which gives rationale for the topic. Clearly stated specific aims.

	Low/Poor	Medium/Good	High/Excellent
Body – Flow and Layout	The report has little organisation, subtopics reflect different sources rather than topics.	Organised according to topics, questions, methods or directions. Separate sources integrated into sections.	Coherent organisation, cited material related to topic and other cited material.
Body – Critical analysis	Content is superficial and inclusions are descriptive. Specific topics / arguments are missing.	Evidence of broad search and appropriate selection. Descriptive presentation with some critical analysis applied to support the aims of the review.	Comprehensive and systematic search and inclusion of material. Critical analysis of strengths and weaknesses as applied to the topic area.
Evaluation/ Conclusion	No synthesis of information into a conclusion. Concluding remarks repeat literature.	Analysis and synthesis of ideas evident in conclusion, some description of future direction based on literature cited.	Succinct and logical conclusion based on information, showing synthesis of ideas. Gaps in literature identified for future work.
References and Mechanics	Many inconsistencies or errors in referencing and style. Grammatical and spelling errors. Sentence meaning is often confused.	Few inconsistencies in referencing in the correct style. Small grammatical errors or instances of awkward flow/ transition from point to point.	Correct and consistent referencing style without errors. Excellent use of standard academic English.

Kate Edwards

Chapter 2
Short formats

5 Multiple choice questions

Multiple choice questions (MCQs) are a common form of assessment as they are objective (if well written) and can be marked automatically and, therefore, reliably and quickly. As there are a large number of short questions, they can also cover a greater proportion of the syllabus than is possible with many other assessment methods. This makes them a popular choice for large, introductory classes, in which a broad understanding of a full range of module content is desirable. Formative MCQs can also provide students with more frequent feedback than is possible with other kinds of assessment, as the tutor can set up standard comments to explain the answers. Students can use this information to help them decide what further work they need to do. In addition, the tests provide tutors with information on the progress of the whole class so that they can make informed decisions about the focus of remedial lectures and follow-up tutorials.

MCQ formats

At their most basic, MCQs can be simple true or false choices, or require students to select an answer from a limited number of options. All answers should be plausible, and similar to each other in terms of length and level of detail, to avoid strategic guessing. Some MCQs have one correct and several incorrect answers, whereas others invite students to select the 'most correct' answer. This should be clearly indicated to the students in the instructions. Due to these issues, producing a bank of high quality MCQs can be challenging and time consuming. However, this improves with practice, and can be made more efficient by adapting existing questions from past papers. Similarly, many banks of MCQs on common topics are available on the internet or from major publishers to be used or adapted.

Although MCQs are typically considered to test knowledge, it is possible to devise assessments that test comprehension, application, analysis, synthesis, computation, interpretation and reasoning. Such assessments can encourage deeper and more applied learning. For example, students can be asked to make a calculation and select the correct answer from the options, or could be given a number of MCQs based on a short narrative case study or experimental data to test their interpretation of the evidence. Other formats have also been proposed, but it is important to ensure that more complex structures do not become confusing.

For any style of MCQ, the number of answer options provided should be carefully considered. The fewer answer options provided, the more these questions are open to guesswork. Questions should be designed so that the mark that is likely to be gained by guessing (i.e. 100 divided by the number of options) is substantially below the relevant pass mark. If this is not possible, some assessors apply negative marking, in which students are penalised for giving an incorrect answer. This is typically calculated as 1 divided by the number of incorrect answers; for example, if there are four answer options, a student would be penalised -0.33 marks for an incorrect answer. However, there is evidence that negative marking can systematically change test behaviour, particularly in risk-averse students, so it may be prudent instead to simply have four or five well selected choices and allow students to give their best answers to all questions.

Scoring MCQs

As technology develops, the modes available for conducting MCQs are increasing. At the time of writing, the most common remains completion of paper scoring sheets, which are then passed through a scanner. However, there are also options to conduct MCQs online, which can be particularly useful for independent formative tests. Using online MCQs for summative testing can bring challenges, in terms of verifying student identity and preventing the use of restricted materials during the test. These issues can be addressed to a large extent by conducting tests in large computer clusters under controlled conditions, although this relies on the institution having sufficiently large facilities for simultaneous testing.

Similarly, MCQs can now be conducted using 'clicker' technology in lecture theatres, in which students use individually identifiable handheld audience response devices to answer questions displayed on the projector. Again, there are some difficulties in using these for summative tests; for example, the requirement to answer questions in the same order at the same pace prevents students from revisiting questions they find difficult. However, they are useful for providing a quick opportunity for students to reflect on learning during a teaching session, and to give the tutor some feedback about the level of understanding on a particular topic. As the technology advances, both online and clicker-based MCQs have the potential to allow effective assessment on both campus-based and distance learning courses.

6 Short answer questions

Short answer questions are used extensively in many subjects. Their brevity allows the coverage of lots of topics in one test, and therefore assessment of multiple learning outcomes. Similarly, short answer questions are mostly designed as objective tests, in which answers are defined relatively easily as correct or incorrect. Thus, other advantages of short answer questions are the speed, ease and reliability of marking. This is particularly true with online tests, where many question designs allow marking by computer alone. As well as efficiency, this has benefits for rapid student feedback and self-assessment (see items **44** and **47**). However, care must always be taken to include every possible iteration of the correct answer, and manual checking may be necessary at times.

Testing knowledge vs. comprehension

Short answer questions are a useful way to assess specific knowledge, and are useful in settings where a substantial body of information needs to be learned by rote. However, it is also possible to devise short answer questions which assess comprehension, application, analysis, synthesis, computation, interpretation and reasoning and yet which are still easily marked.

Types of short answer questions: knowledge recall

Definition questions

For these questions, students are asked to simply define a term or concept. These can involve matching a given term with the appropriate definition from a list, or asking the student to generate the definition from the term or vice versa.

Q. What is the term for a two-dimensional, mirror-symmetrical curve?

Example questions

These questions ask students to state one or more *specific*, real-world instances of some concept. There will be a selection of possible correct answers.

Q. Give an example of a coding language used for web design.

List questions

Students are asked to briefly note or state specific information in a list format.

Q. List the current permanent members of the UN Security Council.

Types of short answer questions: Comprehension

Explanation questions

For these questions, students need to explain *why* something is true or *how* something works. The depth/number of aspects required in answers are often indicated by the number of marks available. The mark scheme would cover quite specific points that should be included.

Q. Explain why confidence intervals are important in reporting summary data.

'Discuss' questions

These questions ask students to point out important features and make a critical judgement. Again, marks would be awarded for mentioning a series of identified key points. Unlike in an essay, there is rarely credit given for more original observations in this style of question, although this could be built into the mark scheme if desired.

Q. Discuss the evidence, or lack thereof, for Maslow's hierarchy of needs.

Relationship questions

Students are asked to state how two or more things relate to each other. Are they opposites? Are they the same thing? Is one an example of the other? How do they differ?

Q. In a competitive market economy, what is the relationship between prices and scarcity?

Calculation questions

For these questions, students need to calculate a numerical answer or answers.

Q. A racing driver drives a car around a circular part of a flat track at a speed of 150km/hr. If the driver experiences a force corresponding to an acceleration of 0.3g in the horizontal direction, what is the radius of the track?

Graphing questions

Students are asked to use a graphical representation for their answer. These usually require accurate labelling of axes and curves.

Q. Draw three graphs to illustrate the changes in heart rate, cardiac output and mean arterial pressure over time for a 22-year-old male endurance athlete who rests for 5 minutes, then cycles at 100W for 5 minutes.

Using alternative formats

Short answer questions are most often answered in a confined space (e.g. one to three lines of text), but different formats may also be considered. 'Fill in the blank' questions are useful for definition and example questions, and matching or ordering can be used for both knowledge recall and comprehension, depending on the test design.

Kate Edwards

Chapter 3
Projects and laboratory classes

7 Laboratory report

Practical classes are an integral part of many subjects, and provide capacity for huge variety in assessments. In some subjects, the performance of the skill itself must be assessed (see item **13**); in others, the collected observations provide the opportunity for assessment of data presentation, analysis and evaluation in the form of a lab report.

A traditional lab report

A traditional experimental lab report usually follows a familiar format. Students are asked to state a problem and hypothesise a possible solution, describe their materials and the methods of their experiment addressing the problem, report their findings, and finally draw conclusions, discussing their hypothesis and the evidence that they generated.

The benefit of attaching assessment to practical classes as a lab report is its potential to improve student engagement with the material. Students who participate in some form of analysis of their practical work will reflect not only on their practical skills but also on integrating this experience with taught material. This helps support the development of deeper understanding. In lab reports, students develop skills of critical evaluation, data presentation and analysis as well as extended writing.

However, traditional lab reports can be onerous for both students and assessors, especially in large cohorts with multiple practical classes. One way around this is to ask students to complete only one section of the report each week. For example, for one lab class they might complete a method section, and then for another just complete a results section. An alternative approach is using a spreadsheet-based lab report, which addresses many of these issues, provides an objective assessment procedure, and develops computer literacy.

A spreadsheet-based lab report

A spreadsheet is any sort of interactive program which organises data into tabular form and allows analysis and graphical displays. A spreadsheet report can be used as an alternative to the traditional format of a lab report, by requiring completion of a series of data presentation and analysis tasks. At lower levels, the tasks could involve completing predesigned tables of data and creating graphs of dependent and independent variables. Students can also be asked to use formulas and linked cells to perform calculations including means and measures of variation, at lower levels, and tests of differences or relationships at more advanced levels. By requiring the students to put specific answers in specific cells, the marking can be quick and objective. A spreadsheet report can also be designed to test theoretical knowledge. For example, comprehension aspects can be done through multiple choice questions from drop down menus, or word-count restricted short answer questions, which allow the assessment of overall concepts that would normally be found in the discussion section of a traditional report.

Improving skills by comparison of data

In any lab report format, in addition to presenting their own data, students can be asked to compare their data to a set generated by the whole class and/or with established data patterns. This activity asks students to think about their data collection performance and explain reasons for their own data (in)accuracies. This self-feedback system will encourage improved future practical skill performance, and help tutors encourage accuracy of measurement.

Kate Edwards

8 Laboratory notes

Assessing laboratory notes encourages a more scientific approach to experimental work and introduces students to the norms of scientific practice. In contrast to experienced scientists who make detailed notes during experimental work, students tend to make few and scrappy notes, which can make it difficult to write the subsequent report. This lack of note-taking may result from poor observation, or may even cause it: if observations have no apparent immediate function, then there is little point carefully recording them. Another possible effect of focussing on the end product, rather than the process, is that students tend to work quickly during laboratory classes, noticing less about what is going on, and reflecting less on this. They follow instructions and adopt a narrow technical approach rather than a wider scientific approach to experimental work.

By assessing the notes written in the laboratory, students are likely to work more systematically, and may try to make more sense of what they are doing as they are completing the experiment. They may also make more observations and record these in better organised notes, and take more care when recording data. Obvious errors are more likely to be picked up, especially if calculations are undertaken immediately, and there may even be the opportunity to do the work again and correct it.

Students can be required to hand in their notes at the end of the laboratory (as an 'instant' lab report), or to compile their work as a laboratory notebook that is assessed as a whole. In both cases, students will need guidance, including the provision of specific headings, good examples, and clear assessment criteria. It should be noted that the quality of presentation is likely to suffer when notes are written in the laboratory. Tutors should make allowance for this and change the assessment criteria so that full and accurate recording of procedures, results, and other observations carries more weight than neatness of presentation.

Instant laboratory reports

An instant lab report, handed in at the end of the class itself, is then either marked immediately in person, or shortly after. This facilitates quick feedback to the students, which can then feedforward into their next laboratory class (see **42**). Structure and presentation of the work can be assisted by giving the students handouts, with spaces to record procedures and results, and to answer brief questions. They can also be provided with graph paper, or computer facilities, for basic plotting of data. Initially it may be necessary to produce a handout specific to the experiment being undertaken, with standard details (e.g. materials and methods) typed in, and only a small number of sections for the students to complete, but the amount of material on the handout can be reduced over time as students become more competent at writing their own laboratory notes. As well as benefiting the students, this approach also saves the tutor's marking time, as instant lab reports tend to be much shorter than those written afterwards.

Laboratory notebook

This is a collection of notes made 'live' in the laboratory but assessed as a whole later in the term. As such, it is tempting for students to complete neater second drafts after the laboratory, which is contrary to the intention of this type of assessment. This can be prevented by providing students with one standard notebook, with fixed pages, that is the only accepted format for use in the laboratory and for later submission. Although this doesn't prevent the addition of later details, it does preclude major revisions and deletions. This is also in accordance with the practice of professional scientists who must keep contemporaneous notes of their work without post hoc additions.

If the laboratory notebooks are submitted after a few classes, the tutor can give some formative feedback. Alternatively, formal viewings, such as an exhibition of student notebooks, can be conducted half way through the year (see item **11**). Such activities help to shape students' future work and encourage learning from peers' good practice.

Apart from its clear benefits to learning during laboratory classes, this method frees students afterwards to do something more constructive than redraft their notes. For example, laboratory notebooks can be used to record subsequent thoughts derived from further reading, analysis of data, seminars and so on. The notebook then becomes a record of the development of students' understanding of the subject, and can be used as the basis for reflection (see item **26**). You could suggest that two pages headed 'thoughts' or 'discussion' be left blank between experiments, to be completed at a later stage as ideas arise.

9 Project report

Final year undergraduates are often asked to conduct a large data-driven research project, either individually or in small groups. This provides the opportunity for a more in-depth consideration of an area of interest, and for the development of appropriate research, statistical and/or technical skills. Although some aspects of this work can be assessed by presentation, poster or contribution to the group (see items **10**, **11**, and **30–32**), the majority of the mark is usually derived from a formal project report.

The structure of a project report usually mirrors that of an academic publication. For example, in the sciences, this is likely to comprise: an introduction which demonstrates a critical understanding of the literature; a method section that outlines the techniques used; a results section which presents and analyses accurate and reliable data in a systematic way; and a discussion section which interprets the results and places them in the context of the extant literature. However, there may also be some additional requirements, such as sections justifying their choice of methodology. Once ready to submit, students can also be asked to use the author guidelines for a particular journal to prepare their submission, in terms of the overall structure, text formatting requirements and referencing style. This increases students' understanding of these conventions, and creates a sense that they are producing a 'real' piece of work.

As project reports are usually the most substantial and independent piece of work that a student completes, it is important that the criteria and process are rigorous. This can be a challenge, as there are usually multiple members of staff involved in supervision and assessment, and projects can vary markedly in their structure and approach. The main areas to consider are the supervisory levels that a student can expect during the project, the marking procedures of the report itself, and education about academic misconduct.

Staff support

The first consideration is ensuring that staff are competent to support the proposed research project. Although most academics would be expected to be able to supervise a piece of work at this level, there are times when a student wishes to pursue a subject that is well outside of the expertise of their allocated supervisor. There should be clear processes in place for students to either change supervisor if necessary, or to refine their project proposal to stay within the expertise of the available staff.

Staff may also have different beliefs about the level of support that it is appropriate to give students. While there will inevitably be variation, given different styles and personalities, it is important to have some general guidance to help standardise between students. For example, it is sensible to stipulate whether staff are allowed to provide formative feedback on drafts prior to submission; this can be a useful opportunity to get personalised feedback on writing, but must be controlled to ensure fairness. Staff may agree that each section of the project report can receive formative feedback once, but no more; this allows for students to get iterative feedback to develop their writing, but without receiving excessive input on any one section. It also encourages students to start writing early, as each section would be submitted for comments in turn. However, it is useful to leave one section (for example the discussion) to be entirely the student's own work with no formative feedback provided, so that their independent work can be assessed.

Another approach to standardising the support available is to provide generic lectures on the key aspects of producing a project report. These could be made available at appropriate times during the year, and include discussions of how to read papers effectively and efficiently, how to manage the writing process, and a reminder about appropriate analytical techniques. As well as helping to ensure that all students have access to at least a basic level of input, this also reduces the amount of time each supervisor needs to spend going through these matters with their small group or individuals, by centralising some of the provision.

Marking and moderation

Given the large contribution that project reports typically make to degree grade, the marking criteria must be explicit and available for students to explore. This includes basic information about the expected length of the piece and the relative weighting of different sections, but also more complex issues. For example, students are often concerned about whether they will penalised if their data reveal a null finding, or results that don't comply with their expectations or the rest of the field. The mark scheme should make clear that the marks are awarded on the basis of the quality of the work and the appropriate handling of the data, rather than the perceived 'correctness' of the findings themselves. Further, mark schemes should navigate the tricky balance between standardisation and responsivity to inevitable variation in project topics and approaches. It is impossible – and indeed undesirable – to come up with a mark scheme that covers every eventuality; instead, it should provide clarity about the general characteristics upon which the work will be judged and how a decision will be reached.

When the projects are marked, it is good practice to have two independent markers, who then compare their comments and marks and reach an agreed grade. There is some controversy regarding whether it is appropriate for the project supervisor to be one of these markers. On the one hand, the supervisor knows the project and the relevant literature better than anyone else, and is best placed to comment on how much the work reflects the independent input of the student. On the other, this opens up the possibility of bias based on their own perceptions of the student's ability outside of the presented report, and makes anonymous marking virtually impossible. It is for individual departments and universities to weigh up the pros and cons of each approach. What is always clear, though, is that a clear record of how marks were determined should be maintained for quality assurance and audit purposes.

Academic misconduct

As projects usually require students to undertake independent data collection, it is important that students are educated about academic misconduct. This includes ethical considerations surrounding the data collection if appropriate, and the importance of accurate, valid measurement, as well as the possible consequences of data fabrication (see item **52**).

Chapter 4
Live assessment

10 Presentations

Presentations are widely used as a basis for assessment in higher education, partly because students and tutors realise that public speaking is a key professional skill to master, but also because they encompass a number of graduate-level competencies. These include: the ability to research a topic and formulate a logical, clear summary of the findings; technical skills, such as timekeeping, material and/or data selection, slide design and software use; communication skills such as confidence, audience engagement, professional behaviour, and responding to questions; and the skills to critically evaluate evidence.

Students entering university are often not experienced in giving presentations, and can be nervous at the prospect of being assessed in this way. However, with appropriate support, most students learn to be comfortable and successful in this environment.

Start early

Presentations can be introduced gradually, as a relatively minor component of in-course assessment in the first year of university. These are often short talks (~5 minutes), given to small groups (~12 students) to create a supportive environment, and on topics that require minimal research. Clear, written guidelines and a discussion of the elements of the presentation prior to the assessment help to reduce student anxiety. This support can be quite prescriptive – such as specifying the number, format and layout of slides (e.g. title and summary slides, use of figures, text, etc.), giving tips on timekeeping and how to avoid needing notes, and so on.

Be clear about the assessment criteria

The assessment criteria should critically align with the learning outcomes provided to the students. For example, the relative weight given to understanding and summarising a topic, personal presentation skills, or critical evaluation may change between the first and final year of the course. This should be explained to students to guide their effort. In addition, assessing 'audience participation', as well as the presentations themselves, appears to increase the engagement of the student audience and the number and quality of questions. These criteria should be set at an appropriate level, in terms of the complexity, range of sources, and level of critical evaluation that is expected of both presenters and the audience.

Consider the level of critical input from staff

Receiving critical feedback can always be challenging and this is exacerbated if the feedback is given in public. Students are often unused to academic discourse and may find well-intentioned questioning intimidating. This should be kept in mind when responding to student presentations, particularly at lower levels. Similarly, it is clear that incorrect answers to questions need to be clarified but handled appropriately so as not to embarrass the student. Sometimes, adding an element of fun, such as framing the assessment panel as the popular TV format 'dragon's den' (or e.g. shark tank/lion's den, depending on location), allows more direct, or indeed combative, questioning without students interpreting it as unfair or intimidating.

Karl Nightingale

11 Exhibitions and poster presentations

Exhibitions can display students' ability to produce artwork or designs (e.g. creative arts) or working examples or models (e.g. engineering, architecture). In the sciences, students may instead exhibit scientific posters which introduce and explain experimental data (e.g. biology, chemistry). All these approaches require a range of technical and communication skills, and provide an authentic and relevant experience of professional practice. Students inspect each other's work, discuss their ideas, and share their enthusiasm. In addition, introducing an external audience by inviting other students, staff members, relevant experts, or members of the public will also increase the authenticity of the situation, and allow students to develop their understanding and their communication skills in a challenging, yet supportive and fun, learning environment.

Establish the marking criteria

This will vary by discipline. In visual arts courses, where students mount exhibitions of their finished work, the focus on the range and quality of the artwork presented may have a greater weight than any supporting presentation. In contrast, in poster presentations, the poster is only a vehicle to convey a student's understanding of a topic, often demonstrated by a short oral presentation where the student 'talks to' or explains the poster. In this case, the technical skills involved in generating the poster (e.g. clarity, illustration, etc.), are important, but the demonstrated understanding of the underlying research and communication skills are often the major focus of the assessment. An example of a scientific poster mark scheme is shown below, which outlines the different aspects that can be assessed.

	Poster content (25%)	Poster appearance (15%)	Presentation of poster (30%)	Answering questions (30%)
A (1st)*	All material is relevant, accurate, clearly described, and shows good evidence of independent thought.	All material is presented in an imaginative, attractive, organised, clear, tidy and professional way. Colour choices aid understanding of the material. Excellent use of images and diagrams to reinforce written material.	Demonstrates excellent understanding of the subject area. Includes appropriate material, which is explained at an appropriate level for the audience. Engaging, entertaining, and easy to follow.	Demonstrates excellent understanding of a broad range of questions. Expands on the answers where appropriate, providing an excellent level of detail. Shows understanding of wider implications.
B (2:1)*	Most material is relevant, accurate, clearly described, with some evidence of independent thought. Occasionally too much or too little detail, or minor errors.	Most material is presented in an attractive, organised, clear, tidy and professional way. Good use of images and diagrams to reinforce written material. Occasional lapses in presentation.	Demonstrates good understanding of the subject area. Includes appropriate material, which is mainly explained at an appropriate level for the audience. Clear and easy to follow. Occasional lapses of flow or accuracy.	Demonstrates good understanding of most questions. Can expand on answers to some extent. Provides a good level of detail and some understanding of wider implications.

C (2:2)*	Mainly relevant and accurate material. Some errors or sections with too much or too little detail. Lacks clarity in places. Little evidence of independent thought.	Mainly clearly presented, but some aspects are messy or poorly presented. May contain too much text or images that are poorly chosen or not referred to.	Mainly demonstrates good understanding of the subject area. Includes appropriate material, with occasional irrelevancies or inaccuracies. May be sometimes delivered at an inappropriate level, with some aspects difficult to follow.	Mainly demonstrates good understanding of a more limited range of questions. Less able to expand on answers where necessary, and demonstrates less understanding of wider implications of their answers.
D (3rd)*	Some relevant and accurate material. Regular errors or sections with too much or too little detail. Lacks clarity throughout. No evidence of independent thought.	Many messy or poorly organised aspects. Some attempt to use presentation to aid understanding but with little success.	Demonstrates some understanding of the subject area, but includes many irrelevancies and inaccuracies. Often delivered at an inappropriate level, with many aspects difficult to follow.	Demonstrates some understanding, but provides many inaccurate or incomplete answers. Not able to expand beyond basic answers, with limited wider understanding.
F (Fail)	Very little relevant and accurate material. Errors throughout and an inappropriate level of detail. No evidence of independent thought.	Generally messy presentation, with little thought given to a professional appearance. Design detracts from understanding of material.	Very little understanding of the subject area, with regular irrelevancies and inaccuracies. No consideration of an appropriate level and no clear narrative.	Largely unable to answer questions accurately.

Key: * UK degree classifications

Consider the markers

The communication skills and design components of a piece of work can be difficult to assess objectively; using two markers may help address the more subjective elements of this approach. However, exhibitions and posters are also an opportunity for peer assessment (see item **39**), which is an excellent way to develop students' critical thinking about communication, research and design skills. As students are rarely familiar with the poster format, it is useful to share some good (and/or poor!) examples. This can be used to demonstrate the assessment criteria, and guide students' expectations of their own and/or other group members' work.

Use as a basis for group-work assessment

Developing an idea, or managing the process of creating something new, is often a team effort in professional practice, and the necessary people, teamwork and communication skills can be developed using these approaches. For example, team-based poster presentations can be an enjoyable process for students, with some guidance. For example, it is important to be explicit about your expectations of outcomes and suggest some ways of working effectively. Students are often not used to working in a group or 'project managing' a task. It is useful to provide an initial 'guidelines session' to discuss how the work can be divided among team members, and suggest a timeline for ensuring the project is delivered on time. It is also possible to assess the overall group product, and each individual's work separately, by allocating particular responsibilities to different team members (see Chapter 8).

Karl Nightingale

12 Discussions and debates

Discussions and debates with staff and peers help students to understand and critically appraise material either given in class or through set reading. However, the benefits gained are dependent on the extent to which students prepare for the discussion and are willing to engage. Assessing class discussions can encourage students to prepare and participate appropriately, and to reward students that do so effectively. In this way, assessment is being used to emphasise the importance of this learning opportunity, to develop critical understanding and the skills to articulate this understanding in an appropriate way.

Class discussions

Staff looking to assess contributions to class discussions often come across considerable difficulties in devising a transparent and defensible system. Assessments solely based on records of attendance are straightforward to administer, and constitute a 'minimum' participation, but they do not reflect the extent and quality of the preparation and discussion. More subjective assessments require careful planning to ensure that they meet the expected quality standards.

Designing the discussion activity so that all students have an equal opportunity to contribute is an important first step. For example, giving each student three cards which they then sacrifice each time they make a contribution can help prevent certain students dominating, and encourage the more reserved to contribute in order to 'get rid' of their cards. Any discussion or debate still requires a skilled facilitator, who can build a positive environment for all contributions. It can also be useful to have a separate marker, as maintaining records of contributions is virtually impossible when you are also chairing the discussion.

Video-recording discussions may also be useful for consistency, feedback and record keeping, as it allows different assessors to view the discussions and to review the marks given. It could even be used to facilitate peer assessment, or to support students to engage with their feedback from staff (see items **39** and **46**).

As with any assessment, the marking criteria are crucial. These should make explicit what types of contributions are most valued. Should students be aiming to contribute original ideas and interpretations? Or is accuracy more important? Is the tone of the contribution, and how the students interact with each other going to be considered or is the assessment solely based on quantity of contributions or the content? By stating the expectations, staff are guiding the behaviour of students, and making clear what types of contributions will be rewarded. Even with these structures in place, it is important to note though, that with in-class discussions, it is impossible to conduct anonymous marking and staff must be very aware of the potential for unconscious bias in their assessments (see item **51**).

Online discussions

Transferring discussions to online environments allows for more objective assessment of contributions with accurate attribution of comments. Additionally, it makes timing of contributions more flexible, allowing discussions to be more democratic and inclusive and, if constructed appropriately, they could be marked anonymously. These factors may have particular benefits for students who are more reluctant to contribute in class settings, such as the more introverted, those with English as an additional language, or those who like more time to reflect before stating an opinion.

An online discussion is directed in a similar way to a face-to-face discussion. For example, a topic, question, or series of questions might be set by the tutor, based on materials provided. The degree of structure may vary with groups of students directed to justify or refute a specific argument, or left open with students asked to contribute according to a theme or open ended question. Other formats might include problem-based learning tasks with collaborative groups using discussion to learn about and solve the question, or an evaluation of experiences such as placements.

Creating a discussion forum is possible using many different programs online and many virtual learning environments have inbuilt facility for forums. The ground rules for discussions should be clear at the outset, in terms of the tone of discussion, and the formality of writing expected. Depending on their level and experience, students could be encouraged to self-police the discussion, or it could be more actively managed by staff. Often students appreciate examples of appropriately constructed contributions, especially in contradicting/correcting previous contributions. It is recommended that spelling and grammar are explicitly not assessed in online discussions because of the speed and spontaneity of student posts. However, effective communication usually requires that all participants are equally able to understand and participate, so abbreviations, jargon, and offensive language should not be permitted.

Assessing contributions can be conducted in different ways (from simple quantitative to qualitative assessment) according to the assignment design, duration, course structure and the weighting given. The simplest method is to require a minimum contribution (e.g. length and number of posts), but some level of assessment of the quality of contributions is recommended. If quality is assessed, it is important that students are given a rubric for marking, which considers factors such as the length, clarity, relevance, utility, tone and sophistication of the post.

Self- and peer assessment

Self and peer assessment can be a useful approach to assessing class discussions, if appropriately structured. Students could be asked to select three oral or online contributions that they, or their peers, have made, and outline the point that was made, their reflections on the strengths of the argument, and any different or additional points that they would add in retrospect. This encourages students to make contributions, to consider their merits, to select the most effective, and to reflect further on how their contributions can be improved.

13 Observation

Observation is a common method of assessment in subjects that require students to display professional competencies. For example, trainee teachers will be observed teaching, dental students giving treatments, and physiotherapists completing clinical assessments. This format allows the assessment of specific knowledge in practice, but also of other important skills such as communication and the performance of practical techniques. Occasionally, observation is also used as an assessment method in purely academic courses, such as within scientific or engineering laboratories. Here it can be a useful method to focus students on the process as well as the end product (see item **8**).

There are various ways in which observation is used as an assessment method. In many cases, it is an on-going process throughout a clinical or industrial placement, and is conducted by a combination of academic staff and practitioners 'in the field'. Although clearly important, this can lead to substantial variation between student experiences; students can only demonstrate some skills if particular situations (e.g. interesting clinical cases, difficult classroom behaviours) present themselves during the observation. There can also be variation in the expectations and marking styles of the staff involved, and it is clearly impossible to anonymise marking to avoid unconscious bias. Assessment of placement performance is discussed in more detail in item **28**.

In other settings, observation is part of the process but only informally affects assessment. For example, in studio-based work (e.g. art, design, architecture) the tutor will spend a lot of time observing the students working, but the assessment is, ostensibly, only of the end product, such as the sculpture, designs, or plans. However, the final assessments are bound to be strongly influenced by the observations the tutor has made of the way these products were arrived at. It might be fairer in such circumstances to be explicit about the role of observation and about the criteria actually being used (for example, speed of working, ability to learn from mistakes, use of equipment). If so, these criteria should be listed for students to see, to make them aware of what the observation consists of and to encourage better practice (see items **41** and **49**).

Finally, some courses have introduced more structured, standardised observation assessments to address some of these issues. For example, in the health sciences, it is common to use Objective Structured Clinical Examinations (OSCEs) as a form of assessment. These involve multiple 'stations' through which the students rotate and are observed. At each, they encounter a different clinical scenario, and are asked to perform an exam, make a diagnosis, demonstrate a technique, or deliver bad news to a patient. This provides all students with the same opportunities, and allows the same assessor to assess all students on a particular scenario. By marking against a standardised list of specific behaviours, these short tests can be marked relatively objectively by trained assessors. The use of actors as simulated patients, or even real patient volunteers, adds to the validity of the process and, if appropriate, their reflections can influence the marks given. As OSCEs are still live assessments, they cannot eliminate the influence of unconscious bias noted previously. However, by having multiple assessors the effects of individual prejudices are minimised. Similarly, the structured environment provides the opportunity to video record the assessment for moderation purposes. Although OSCEs can be relatively labour intensive, they could be a viable alternative to more traditional written assessments in other academic disciplines.

14 Viva

The viva, or oral exam, is most commonly used to assess:

- Oral fluency and comprehension (e.g. in language learning);
- Personal qualities, attitudes, or interpersonal skills (e.g. in admissions, or professional training);
- The ability to critically evaluate and diagnose problems in novel situations (e.g. clinical training);
- Work previously submitted (e.g. a dissertation, design, or recording of a musical performance) to ensure the candidate is the author of the submitted work, and to further explore understanding.

A viva can also be used for individuals or small groups who lack writing skills, who miss final exams through illness, or whose marks fall on the borderline between two degree grades.

The flexibility of the viva is its great advantage. Issues can be explored in depth, in a 'bespoke' manner, which is not possible in other forms of assessment based on posing fixed questions to all students. Even a short viva can give a rich impression of the candidate's breadth and depth of understanding. However, this flexibility is also why this can be a stressful approach for students. The viva is not used widely in secondary education, and students are unfamiliar with the format. Likewise, its potential to be both wide-ranging and/or focus in on detail – to 'expose' ignorance or misunderstanding – is a frequent area of concern. Rumours of combative or 'unreasonable' examiners do little to reduce anxiety. Because of the potential problems, the viva is often used in conjunction with other assessment methods to increase the range of information available about a candidate, or the work. This can be done in a variety of ways:

- a brief viva after reading an essay, but before allocating a mark;
- a brief viva focussing on the context/problems experienced during practical or project work (these are rarely described in assessed reports), before allocating a mark;
- a viva as a preparation for other forms of assessment. These aim to identify and diagnose weaknesses which require further attention;
- a viva during laboratory work, to assess students' understanding and encourage critical evaluation of the project.

Choice of examiners

Viva examiners should be expert in the field, experienced in what can be reasonably expected from students at this level, and have an appropriate temperament (i.e. calm, flexible, persistent). This can be a rare combination of skills and expertise. Using two examiners can have practical advantages, allowing one to take a more active role as questioner, while the other observes and evaluates. Having two examiners also helps when justifying the validity of a decision afterwards. Defence of viva decisions in the face of appeals tends to be based on the status and reputation of the examiner. A chairperson, who acts as an independent observer to oversee the process and its alignment with university policy, is also a useful addition, particularly where the viva forms a substantial component of assessment.

Examiner preparation

It is also important to ensure that examiners are well informed about the nature and purpose of the viva. If the examiner is not the main tutor on the module, then they should be told what the learning outcomes are, what material the students have received, and the expected level of performance (i.e. their year of study and the amount of preparation they are expected to have completed). This enables examiners to structure their questioning strategically, and ensure that all students have an appropriate viva experience.

Reducing student stress

Examiners need to minimise the stress of the approach, to ensure that candidates perform at their best. This requires maintaining a balance between keeping the candidate relaxed and asking challenging questions, and directing the viva to particular areas if necessary. There are number of practical approaches to minimising anxiety:

- Make the process as transparent as possible. Prior to the viva, tell the students who the examiners are, why they are appropriate assessors, and the expected duration and scope of the assessment.
- At the outset, briefly explain how the viva will work, and how the student should proceed if unsure (ask examiner to rephrase a question, break question into parts, etc.).
- Attempt to put the candidate at ease. For example, it can help, if the work is a clear pass, to tell them so at the start. Many examiners start with a straightforward question that allows the student to put their case (e.g. Can you summarise what you have shown? If you had the time again, what would you do differently?). These questions can naturally lead to more challenging topics.

Karl Nightingale

Chapter 5
Problem-based assessment

15 Comprehension tasks

In comprehension tasks, students are given a case study, extract of text, or some data, and asked to respond appropriately. This requires students to undertake an analysis 'live' and prevents the regurgitated answers sometimes provided in response to more standard essay questions (see item **2**). These types of questions are common in literature-based subjects, in which short extracts of text are given for analysis, but can also be used in a variety of other disciplines.

Literature and language

Here students are asked to engage with a provided extract, and to produce an appropriate commentary. This can be focussed primarily on a detailed analysis of the text itself, or can use the extract to frame a more general discussion of the wider research context. For example:

Q. Discuss the vocabulary choices in each text, and compare the two texts in relation to their styles and communicative objectives. Base your answer on a close analysis of features of the two texts.

Q. With reference to the extract below, interrogate the relationship between race and the broader ideologies that underpinned empire in the period. Make sure you discuss the work of at least two writers from the course.

Experimental data

In science and engineering, results from an experiment could be provided as a table or graph, with the students asked to describe the observed results, discuss their implications, and put them in the context of recent literature.

Q. What light does the following experimental evidence throw on Triesman's model of selective attention?

Role play

Students can be given a description of a particular scenario and asked to provide a written response as an appropriate professional. Such questions help them to see the relevance of the task and to take a personal interest in it. Their writing often becomes more natural and fluent. There is of course a danger of encouraging too flippant an approach but this can be kept in check by ensuring the question requests a formal response.

Q. Your client has inherited his late aunt's urban estate under her will and is considering whether it would be more profitable to sell the property quickly or 'sit and speculate'. Discuss the factors you would consider in reaching a recommendation.

Hypothesis formation

Here students are asked to speculate about outcomes of particular scenarios, based on their theoretical understanding and knowledge of past precedent. This again encourages the practical application of learning to a novel context and enables students to demonstrate their understanding of different perspectives.

Q. Attached is a planning proposal for a new shopping precinct in a suburban area. Speculate about any likely planning objections raised to these plans by (a) the local community and (b) the planning officer.

16 Design tasks

Whereas comprehension tasks (see item **15**) ask students to respond appropriately to existing materials, design tasks instead require students to come up with their own creative solutions to particular challenges. These assess innovation and decision making, as well as students' ability to apply their theoretical understanding to real-life situations. Such questions are common in subjects such as architecture and urban planning, but can be easily adapted to other scenarios. Tasks could include: writing grant applications for scientific studies; designing a teaching session; developing marketing materials; creating judging criteria for a literary award; an engineering task, or a public health campaign. For example:

Q. Given the street plans, existing locations of shops, site values and other information in the appendices, design and site a new small shopping precinct and justify your major decisions.

Q. Design an experiment to test the duration of short-term memory for verbal items following different kinds of initial information processing, and justify your major decisions.

Q. Design a video aimed at changing smoking behaviour based on the theory of planned behaviour. Explain how it addresses the major tenets of the theory, and the evidence that an intervention of this nature is likely to be successful.

Asking students to justify their methodological decisions, in light of current research, can be particularly useful to explore understanding. This can be unstructured, as above, or guided through a series of sections, as illustrated in the example below.

Q. Your local hospital has access to 1000 breast cancer patients, and is particularly interested in how exercise can influence health in this population. Design an appropriate experiment and justify this research approach with reference to existing literature and clinical priorities.

- Discuss the wider context and literature as background to the study. It is important to identify the novelty and importance of the proposed study (30% of marks).
- Describe the aims and design of your study, including justification of the methods and research design chosen (35% of marks).
- Outline your hypothesised results based on previous research (15% of marks).
- Discuss any ethical issues and actions taken to address these (10% of marks).
- Give a brief description and justification of the statistical analyses used to address your hypotheses (10% of marks).

These assignments can also be made more experiential by inviting local employers to present a real-life scenario for which the students are required to present a possible solution. This adds meaning to the assignment and help students to develop relevant employability skills. It also builds relationships between local businesses and the university, as the students will usually come up with creative and viable propositions that could be taken forward (see item **18**).

17 Calculation tasks

A critical skill for any student of science or engineering is to draw sound conclusions from data. This allows a student to make claims based on evidence, which should be reproducible by others at a later time from the same data. Such a skill requires the student to get used to manipulating data whilst keeping an 'audit trail' of their actions. It also involves taking procedures/formulae that they observe in the work of others, and being able to apply them to their own data.

Examples of a calculation assignment would be to provide some data, and a set of instructions or formulae, and require the student to compute some (known) value. Spreadsheet applications are an invaluable resource in this respect, as they make it relatively easy to implement quite complex calculations. Care should be taken when marking calculation assignments if the correct result is a single number. It is tempting to apply automated marking procedures, or simply to scan the answer looking for what you know to be the 'correct' result. However, the student's answer may be valid but computed in a subtly different way than you expected – for example, computing something in a different logarithm base, or a value as a fraction, or to a smaller number of decimal places than you were expecting. Wherever possible, therefore, the calculations should be structured in small stages, each stage requiring a particular output. This has the further benefit that even if the wrong answer is computed at an early stage, 'method marks' can be awarded by looking at the methodology employed at each stage.

Interesting variants can also be set, where one student must write a set of instructions/formulae for another student to reproduce. Alternatively, a larger set of data can be provided, and the students asked to pick out the particular elements they need to perform the requested calculation, discarding the rest. To increase the difficulty of the task, and the real-world applicability, students could also be given a more narrative problem, and a dataset, and asked to identify and perform the necessary calculations to answer the problem. This not only requires students to be able to perform a calculation but also to select the appropriate calculations that need to be performed. With any of these formats, it is relatively easy to swap in a new set of data/numbers, so there are effectively an infinite number of possible questions, changing every year.

Gavin Brown

Chapter 6
Authentic assessment

18 Introducing authentic assessment

Authentic assessments involve meaningful 'real-life' problems or tasks. Rather than only assessing whether students have acquired the appropriate knowledge and skills, authentic assessments explore the students' application of these abilities to particular situations. They thereby assess the integrated performance of a student, and explore their level of mastery or capability. There are likely to be multiple solutions to an authentic assessment, so students are able to demonstrate their creativity and innovation, as well as the required knowledge and skills.

Authentic assessments are most effective when the task and its environment are as close as possible to a real life situation. For this reason, many universities using these assessments will build partnerships with local business or community organisations, who then present a particular challenge that they are having to the students. The students are then asked to explore the possible options, and present their proposed solution to the organisation. Staff from the organisation could even provide input to the feedback and/or the marks given to the students.

Introducing authentic assessment requires a different approach to curriculum planning to more traditional assessments. Typically an educator would start with planning what content they want to include in the course, and then design an assessment that tests the extent to which students have mastered this content. In contrast, a course based on authentic assessment would start with the question: What do we want students to be able to do at the end of this course? They would then plan the curriculum to ensure that students have the appropriate knowledge, skills, and experiences to complete these tasks.

This type of assessment has many benefits. Students are likely to see the relevance of the activities more readily, and this can enhance their engagement. By having to apply their learning, rather than just repeat it, authentic assessments help students identify gaps in their knowledge, understanding or skills and then provide the impetus to remedy this. They also provide concrete examples of how courses develop graduate employability, which is highly relevant for students, parents, and external stakeholders such as employers.

This chapter outlines a range of activities that could be introduced as authentic assessments. However, there are many other styles of assessment covered elsewhere in this book that could also be adapted to be made more authentic. For example, laboratory reports could address a real life question, and calculation or design assignments linked to a local community project.

19 Writing for public dissemination

Creating impact from research is an increasing priority in academia and society as a whole, but students have few opportunities to develop the skills to communicate complex ideas to a general audience effectively. This is unfortunate, as many students will go on to careers in which they will, in some way, need to translate specialist information for a wider audience. Designing assessments where students are asked to write for the public is one way to address this issue. This type of work encourages them to think about how to make ideas and language both accessible and engaging for non-specialist audiences. From a cognitive perspective, such tasks also require students to pick out the key aspects of a piece of research or topic and to identify the broader implications of the work for society.

For example, students can be asked to select a recent piece of research from a relevant area, and write a short lay article about it. Alternatively, the assessment could ask for an opinion piece on a controversial topic, in which the student needs to argue a particular viewpoint backed up by appropriate, and well explained, evidence. In both examples, the choice of target publication is important to encourage intelligent but non-specialist articles, and avoid more sensationalist approaches. Sensible options include good quality newspapers or appropriate periodicals.

As this is likely to be a relatively novel task for students, it would be appropriate to provide support in advance through seminars or workshops. To generate examples, it is useful to ask students to analyse existing examples of work (e.g. newspaper articles and their corresponding original journal article), to explore how the language, style, and content of media pieces differ from their academic equivalents. These workshops can also incorporate elements of peer feedback (see item **39**) to help them further develop their ideas and approaches.

Once complete, assessments of this nature form a useful resource for the students; you essentially have a series of easily understood summaries of key aspects of research. With appropriate permission from the students, you could circulate this work to the rest of the cohort to broaden understanding and aid preparation for future assessments.

20 Writing for the Internet

Publishing materials on the internet has become accessible to all, due to the development of straightforward and freely available online editing and dissemination platforms. This has opened up a new sphere of assessment, in which students are asked to produce a variety of materials for online publication and to engage in online interactions. As well as developing the general skills of writing for a wider audience outlined in item **19**, this approach also helps students to develop some technical skills that could be useful in future employment. This does mean that some support should be provided initially, as students will vary in their previous experience.

Another key feature of this type of assessment is the knowledge that any online work may be read by staff, fellow students, and members of the public. Awareness of this increases motivation, by creating a broader purpose to the assessment. The possibility of outside evaluation can also develop a sense of ownership, and encourage students to produce higher quality work. At the same time, the public forum may invoke some anxiety and a reluctance to engage for fear of judgement. This should be explicitly discussed with students, so that they have the opportunity to express and resolve any concerns. Ultimately they must also have the option not to publish their work online, or to do so anonymously, as there are many valid reasons why a student may not feel comfortable to do so. In these circumstances, offline replicas of an online resource can be assessed as an alternative.

This public forum also raises issues of accountability and confidentiality. Time must be taken to consider how poor quality (spelling, grammar, content) or inappropriate posts will be managed, and the workload associated with this task. It may be possible to introduce peer monitoring, in which students can anonymously flag posts from others that they are concerned about or that they believe require review. Although addressing this issue can be challenging, it can be a good opportunity to discuss ethical issues surrounding the balance between freedom of expression and the protection of individual and institutional reputations.

Developing online materials also helps students to interact with each other and with the wider world, through the production of joint content and/or engagement in online discussions. This requires students to express their opinions, and respond appropriately to the opinions of others in a community of learning. There is also the scope for students to raise their public profiles and to forge real-life collaborations or links with organisations and potential employers. In addition, selecting appropriate hyperlinks for inclusion in their materials can also encourage wider reading and critical appraisal of sources, and helps students to place their knowledge in a broader context.

As with any assessment, it is crucial to be explicit about the marking criteria. This may include specifying the number and quality of expected posts or contributions, and giving information on the weighting of content quality against other factors such as appearance, creativity, profile generated and so on. In particular, if the purpose is to engage deeper academic engagement, as well as the production of more populist and/or opinion-based materials, then the marking criteria should emphasise the use of appropriate theories and evidence in content and discussions.

Wikis

A wiki is a collaborative writing space with multiple authors. Wikipedia has popularised the format, making it a familiar concept for students. Wikis can be incorporated into assessment either by asking students to review and edit existing wikis for accuracy and content, or by asking them to produce their own wiki on a particular topic. The facility to edit contributions makes a wiki a useful tool, as material can be updated and evaluated over time, in particular as students develop their critical thinking. In addition, the software can track the unique contributions of each individual, allowing for more individual assessment. The tasks can also be made more authentic, by emphasising how the finished product will be a valuable revision tool for the whole class, or useful for the general public.

Working together in groups on a wiki provides students with the opportunity to compare their learning to that of others, and to help clarify each other's thoughts. However, it may be challenging, particular where there are disagreements. This is exacerbated by the freedom that all participants have to change the text and delete the work of others. Students may need support to determine how best to negotiate these differences and produce an agreed final piece of work. Staff input, to correct or confirm responses, may be necessary at this point, or later when wikis are released as learning materials for others.

Blogs

Blogs are a form of frequently updated, chronological micro-publishing, in which the 'blogger' writes about particular topics, makes personal observations, and often reviews and provides links to external sites. There is usually a platform in which readers can also comment on the blog and engage in ongoing discussions. In terms of assessment, student bloggers can be asked to write and publish individual reflections on learning, or to produce more outward-facing commentaries or opinion pieces on particular issues.

It is relatively straightforward for even novices to get started, and the requirement to write regularly for the public can help develop writing fluency. The comments function also encourages a dialogue between the reader and the blogger, and helps students to develop the skills to interact appropriately with those in the wider world, who may have very different views, experiences and approaches.

Where writing for a wider audience, blogs help students to develop their 'voice' and to learn to explain concepts in appropriate levels of detail and in an engaging way. The tone should vary, depending on whether the blog is aimed at the general public, or for a particular professional audience, and this should be made clear in the assessment criteria. At its most extreme level, language students can be required to blog in their second/third language in order to further develop their communication skills.

Where students are reflecting on their own experiences, such as their learning on a placement, blogging also increases a sense of cohort. Students share their own writing, and read that of others, and the comments can foster a sense of a shared experience and provide an opportunity for instrumental and emotional peer support. However, students may need encouragement to value these peer comments, and move away from the perspective that only staff comments and opinion are useful. Blogs can be a useful online tool for presenting portfolios or reflective diaries (see items **25** and **26**).

Other approaches

Online contributions may take advantage of other popular and useful applications. For example, assessments could require students to use Twitter as a communication tool, such as to tweet the key points of lectures or readings. Tweets can then be tracked using class-specific hashtags. This method has the advantage of requiring students to be succinct in their contributions (fewer than 140 characters). Assessing Twitter contributions is most simply done by quantity, but qualitative assessment, although more onerous, is possible either by counting retweets or marking the content of the tweet itself. Other tools include the Up-Goer Five text editor, which requires students to only use the ten hundred (1000) most commonly used words (so, for example, the word 'thousand' is not a permitted word). This encourages students to explain a concept simply and describe it in their own way rather than learning by rote descriptions provided, and adds a fun and challenging slant to an online task.

Kate Edwards and Vikki Burns

21 Creating multimedia materials

It has never been more accessible to create and publish multimedia materials. Relatively ubiquitous technology like smartphones and tablets can make high quality audio and video recordings, complete basic editing, and make them immediately available online. For those with a little more time and expertise, widely available software allows more sophisticated editing and production of professional quality materials. This has opened up many opportunities for specialists, and indeed non-specialists, to communicate with the general public using a whole variety of media. It is clear that having the skills to plan and produce such materials will be important for many modern graduates.

In addition to developing specific skills, creating multimedia materials as an assessment has a number of other benefits. It requires the students to consider which aspects of their learning are relevant for a particular audience, and to think of creative ways to illustrate key concepts. To do so, the students also have to ensure that their own understanding is solid and well evidenced. For example, students could produce a short video or podcast on a particular topic; the potential audience would either be selected by the tutor or left for the student to choose. Similarly the purpose of the piece needs to be clear. It might be to explain a basic theory or idea in an imaginative way, or to summarise the findings of a recent piece of research. Alternatively it may be to give an overview of an area of literature, presenting different perspectives or areas of controversy, or to advocate for one particular viewpoint. All could be valid assessments, depending on the topic and the learning outcomes identified.

As discussed in items **19** and **20**, extra incentives for students can be provided by encouraging them to publish their final submissions online for their peers and the external world to view. This inspires a sense of achievement, creates a set of future learning resources, and gives the students something very tangible to share with future employers or other external bodies. As with other forms of technology though, it is important to provide the students with appropriate support, so that those less familiar with the technical details are not disadvantaged. Depending on the nature of the programme, the tutor may wish to give less or no credit for sophisticated recordings and editing. For example, if the priority is on the choice of topic, and the clarity and accuracy of the message, it may be sensible to stipulate that it should be recorded as a single shot on a basic device with no editing. In contrast, if learning to use appropriate technology is one of the wider skills to be developed in the course, then credit can be given in the mark scheme for excellent use of different shots or editing techniques. As with any assessment, this should be made clear to students in advance in the mark scheme.

22 Designing learning materials

Students are very familiar with using a variety of learning materials, including online resources, lecture notes, encyclopaedia entries, and crib sheets. They are likely, therefore, to have opinions about what features make the most useful learning resources and how they should be written for maximum utility. Further, having to explain a topic to someone else often highlights the student's level of understanding, and encourages them to really clarify their thinking. Taken together, this suggests that designing learning materials for other students provides a useful opportunity for authentic assessment.

For example, students could be asked to adapt existing learning materials for a more novice audience. This requires students to select the most important components to retain and to explore how they could explain them with fewer technical terms and relying on less prior knowledge. Alternatively, the assessment may involve creating a short resource from scratch, such as a diagram that summarises the findings of a recent scientific paper or philosophical theory. At its most authentic, students can redesign the lecture slides for their course, based on their own experience of participating! The work would then be assessed in terms of its accuracy, appropriateness for the audience, creativity and clarity of presentation, and so on.

To heighten the relevance and the authenticity of the assessment, students can be advised from the start that, once completed and marked, their materials will be provided as a resource to their classmates, future classes and/or other appropriate groups. This adds a level of responsibility for the students in terms of assuring the quality of the products, and can often lead to more effort and engagement. However, for the sake of institutional integrity, educators may wish to consider a threshold mark, or level of performance, below which assessments would not be shared publicly. It would also be important to discuss in advance with the students whether they wanted their contributions to be credited or anonymous in this forum.

23 Briefing papers

Briefing papers are commonly written by experts for government ministers or executives in large organisations to ensure that they are up to date with a particular issue. They are relatively short documents that summarise the relevant background, highlight any issues of concern, and will often discuss possible next actions. Authors of briefing papers need to consider carefully not only their topic, but also the recipient of the briefing paper, to ensure that it is focussed, relevant, and in an appropriate level of detail. The papers must be pragmatic, selective and concise. They should also demonstrate how theoretical understanding is relevant to a real-world issue. As such, writing a briefing paper can be a useful assessment for students in a wide variety of subjects.

In these assessments, students are given some background about their proposed recipient and asked to draft a briefing paper on a particular topic. To add to the authenticity, this may be a real person who could come and introduce themselves, explain their role, and what they require from a briefing paper. Alternatively, students can identify their own topic that they believe would be relevant for this person, or indeed identify their own recipient as well as their topic.

As with any novel tasks, students would need support to understand the purpose and structure of a briefing paper. Workshops are a useful way to share some examples and compare their structures and approaches. They should pay particular attention to how a background section for a briefing paper may differ from an introduction to a research paper for example; in a briefing paper, it is unlikely to take a chronological approach and will instead highlight the key events or developments that are crucial for understanding. The approach to giving recommendations should also be made clear. Does the educator want the students to advocate for a particular recommendation, giving the benefits, risks, possible opposing arguments and their counterarguments? Or do they instead want them to provide a range of options, and discuss the advantages and disadvantages of each in turn? Both can be legitimate approaches, but the expectations must be made clear for the student.

To enhance the authenticity of the task, students may be advised that all or some of the briefing papers will be submitted to the intended recipients (for example a local politician) for their consideration. Submission could precede marking and form part of the marking process, or follow marking by sharing a selection of papers as examples of student work.

24 Planning and running events

For some degree programmes, such as hospitality and catering or sports management, planning and running an event can be a key component of assessment. It demonstrates students' ability to take their theoretical learning of project and event management and apply them to a real scenario. However, it is likely that this form of assessment could be useful in other academic disciplines. For example, students of health psychology could be asked to design and run a public event to promote healthy behaviours or smoking cessation, and use psychological theories to justify their design; science students could organise and run a conference or public information event; or business students could design an event to showcase their skills and attributes to local employers in an imaginative and theory-based way.

In some settings, it may not be possible for students to actually run the event in question due to an unsuitable size of cohort, available resources, or ethical constraints. In this scenario, a plan for a hypothetical event can instead form the assessment. For example, it may be difficult for social work students to run real events for ethical reasons, but they could be asked to design an event for prospective adoptive parents to meet children in care, and use evidence and theories to back up their design. Further, art historians could be assessed on their ability to curate their dream exhibition if money and geographical location were no barrier, and to justify their decisions.

Regardless of the nature of the event, there are a variety of ways in which the event and/or event design could be assessed. In the case of actual events, the success of the event itself may be taken into account. It would be important to be clear by what criteria this will be judged. Will it be by the number of people in attendance or other quantifiable measures? Or will it be by a more subjective judgement of its level of sophistication and appropriate use of theories? Another approach to assessing these real events would be the production of reflective diaries (see item **26**), in which students would be asked to discuss their approach to planning the event, the event itself, and to reflect on the success of the event and the processes employed. In the case of hypothetical events, assessment would focus instead on a written event plan, which includes, for example, some background or justification for the event, a detailed plan, and specification of success criteria. The emphasis placed on different aspects, for example the financial planning, would depend on their relevance for the learning outcomes of the module.

Chapter 7
Assessment over time

25 Portfolios

Portfolios are commonly used in the selection, and assessment, of students in art and design-based subjects. In these cases, a student's portfolio will contain sketches, notes and versions of a final product as well as a number of finished pieces, selected from a year's work. However, portfolios can also be used in other subject areas where the assignments are not necessarily visual. Instead of handing in a small number of separate assignments, students produce a portfolio or file containing a larger number of shorter pieces for assessment.

The portfolio method encourages students to work consistently throughout a module; they are producing a series of outputs, evaluating them, and selecting the best – or those that go together to make the best portfolio. In other words, they are charting their own progress on the module, monitoring it and summarising it. This also gives the opportunity for students to be more experimental in their approach (as they can discard less successful pieces), without involving tutors in too much marking.

The portfolio method also lends itself very well to the incorporation of peer feedback opportunities. Interim due dates can be agreed, on which students present their work to one another in small sub-groups, and receive encouragement, criticism and suggestions for improvement. On the basis of this feedback they polish their work and select items for the portfolio, which is submitted on the final due date when it is assessed by the tutor. This also adds an element of self-reflection, as students are also able to track their own progress. They can see how their work has developed over time, and can use this to see how it can be further improved in the future (see item **29**).

26 Reflective diaries

A reflective diary is an individual record in which a student regularly describes her or his thoughts and behaviours either during (reflection-in-action), or after (reflection-on-action), a learning experience. This is often used where the purpose of a module is the students' experience, including more applied modules, field trips, or external opportunities such as placements or internships. This experience is not available from textbooks or lectures and has to be identified by the participants themselves. Similarly, this approach is useful in courses where developing a reflective approach is a key outcome, such as in education or other more vocational courses.

The reflective diary differs from the essay or report in its focus on the process of learning, rather than the outcome, and also in that it tends to be informal in style and structure. However, it is not usually atheoretical; students are encouraged to consider theoretical models and consider how these are reflected in their own personal experiences. Reflective diaries, therefore, encourage students to think critically about their learning, and to use theoretical frameworks to understand and enrich these experiences. Where appropriate, these reflections are then used to consider, and implement, improvements in practice.

As completing a reflective diary can be a novel experience for students, it is important to provide support and guidance about appropriate approaches. Highly structured task instructions are particularly useful for groups who lack experience in this type of work: students are asked to complete a specific form, with guiding questions for each learning experience (many examples of these forms are available online). Alternatively, students may be provided with more open guidance, such as 'Keep a diary in which you write a brief summary of the activities of each session. Say what you have learned about yourself and others, and consider this in the light of appropriate theoretical models [or a named specific theoretical model]'. Whether structured or unstructured, it is important to encourage students to challenge their beliefs and to explore their experiences through a range of 'lenses' or perspectives. This prevents the diary becoming a tool that reinforces set ideas, rather than exploring new ideas.

Supporting workshops can help encourage good practice. Examples of reflective diaries (e.g. from previous cohorts, with permission) can be shared, especially where they demonstrate progress in their thinking over time; the group can then discuss what features made these diaries effective. Similarly, the workshops give an opportunity for peer feedback, in which students read one another's diaries after a few weeks. This helps students to see the potential of the diary form and understand the range of approaches that can be taken. Tutors can also give feedback on an early entry, to ensure that students are on the right track.

A common concern with reflective diaries, for tutors and students alike, is how to assess them transparently and reliably. In actuality, the criteria for assessing diaries can be similar to those for other written work. Though there may be no strict rules about structure or writing style, students can still be judged on such criteria as originality, commitment, and the skills of observation, analysis and synthesis. The priority is to be explicit to students about criteria, and preferably to devise criteria together with students and/or give them the opportunity to apply them to existing diaries, so that they understand the criteria and are committed to them.

A cautionary note to finish is that reflective diaries rely on high levels of trust between tutors and students, and may raise some issues of confidentiality, both in terms of their own disclosures and their discussions of other people. This should be discussed with students early in the process. For example, students should be reassured about where confidentiality applies to their disclosures, but also informed about circumstances in which this may be breached (e.g. if a student discloses information that suggests that they are a risk to themselves or to others). Similarly, it is useful to discuss how and when to either anonymise, or even omit, comments or information about other people. Depending on the nature of the diary, and the number of students, it may also be difficult to retain anonymous marking procedures (see item **51**); this should therefore be addressed in your appropriate quality assurance systems.

27 Diary of an essay

Reflective diaries, as outlined in item **26**, can be combined with more traditional assessments to encourage students to think about how they learn, as well as what they learn. For example, students could be asked to write a short reflective diary about their activities as they go through the process of writing an essay. It would comprise a chronological account of what they did and when, including how they planned their essay, what search terms they used to identify appropriate literature, and what different structural and conceptual iterations they went through before settling on the final piece of work. An e-portfolio is an effective way of presenting a piece of work of this nature, as it could link to draft documents or websites used. The student then receives a mark and feedback on both the essay itself and the diary about the essay-writing process. The relative weightings of these would be dependent on the priorities of the module.

Honesty is crucial in a piece of work like this. It is important to emphasise that marks would be awarded for detailed descriptions of the process, including any late starts and false leads, and then thoughtful reflections on how effective this approach was. This helps avoid students providing a sanitised description of how they wish they had written the essay! However, the process of observation itself may also help the essay writing in the short term. Just knowing that they will have to write down what they did, is likely to encourage students to work in a more organised, thoughtful way.

This type of reflective work encourages students to take a metacognitive approach, in which they think about how they go about writing an essay. In doing so, it introduces or reinforces the notion that you can become better at learning and producing academic work, rather than this being solely driven by ability. If these diaries are then shared with peers, as part of a peer assessment exercise, it provides a valuable insight into how other people study and what practices characterise those who achieve higher grades. In this way, students are sharing good practice, and discussing areas of difficulty about the process of writing itself. This also gives the tutor important information about study habits, which can guide future learning support for the students.

28 Assessing placement performance

It is increasingly common for students to spend a period of time on placement with an employer or organisation as part of their degree programme. These vary from relatively short placements of days or weeks, through to entire years in industry. These may be compulsory parts of the course, such as in clinical or education programmes, or options that students can select. They tend to be popular with students and employers alike, and are a valuable opportunity to apply knowledge to a real-life situation in a supported and guided environment.

However, assessing student performance on placements is very challenging. As well as subject-specific knowledge, the placements are often intended to help develop a range of softer skills, such as professional attributes, diplomacy, project management and communication. These are difficult to assess objectively, particularly where the opportunities for the development and demonstration of these skills can vary markedly between placements. Further, at least some of the marks are usually awarded by staff at the placement site, rather than by university staff, which leaves considerable scope for variation in practice. As these assessments cannot be anonymised, biased marking – whether conscious or unconscious – can be an issue (see item **51**), particularly if there have been problems on the placement.

Structure of the assessment

Assessments of placements can be based on relatively informal observations of the student's work, and how it meets the learning criteria. If this is the case, the criteria must be clearly articulated to both student and assessor so that they understand what will be observed. It is useful for these criteria to align with a professional standards framework, if one exists for the relevant profession;

this means the assessor is likely to be familiar with the criteria and it gives further authenticity to the experience for the student. However, this approach can be problematic; it relies on the assessor being in a position to observe all aspects of performance, which may not be possible due to locations and/or schedules. It further relies on all assessors having adequate training and preparation, and equal understanding of the assessment. It is also open to bias and inconsistency, and can be very hard to moderate in any meaningful way.

Alternative, more structured, approaches can help to address these issues. For example, students could be assessed on the completion of a particular piece of work-based writing, such as a care plan or a design brief. This reduces concerns about the assessor having to observe all aspects of the work, but conversely it does mean that some of the softer skills may receive less attention. University-based assessment of placements is also common, and allows for a greater control as there would be a more limited number of assessors. This could include portfolios, reflective diaries, oral presentations or research reports (items **25**, **26**, **10**, and **9**). Other options include vivas or project exams about the placement experience, in which students are asked to reflect on different experiences (see items **14** and **37**). Any of these assessments may include feedback from service users such as clients or patients of the organisation. It is likely that a combination of these approaches would be the most reliable way of assessing a placement, particularly where it makes a large contribution to the degree grade.

Timing of the assessment

As with any assessment, it is important for students to understand how they are progressing against the learning criteria on their placement. This starts at the very beginning, where it can be helpful for students to complete a learning contract with their university and placement organisation, to ensure that everyone has the same understanding and expectations. After that, opportunities to get feedback should be built into the programme, and timed such that the student can develop and improve based on the feedback given, before their final assessment. This could comprise a series of smaller pieces of summative work, with periods of time in between for students to develop, or some formative feedback prior to the final summative assessment. In addition to giving informal oral feedback, comments should be recorded in writing, to ensure that there are appropriate records.

Responsibilities for assessment

One of the most challenging aspects of assessing placements is the range of people involved and their varied backgrounds and experiences. They are likely to have different opinions about the relative importance of different aspects of placement performance, or about what constitutes a 'good' mark. Historically, for example, some clinical staff have been reluctant to give students higher marks, as 'they still have a lot to learn'. This emphasises the need for appropriate training and guidance, to ensure that regulations and expectations are explicit. Conducting staff marking exercises with placement staff can be very informative (see item **50**), although it can be difficult to organise for everyone to be together at the same time.

If a wide variety of staff are involved in assessment, and especially where they are relatively inexperienced, it may be advisable to use a simpler mark scheme that awards either pass or fail, or pass/merit/distinction. This may be preferable to staff giving actual grades or percentages if they lack comparators to award these in a reliable way. This is common in vocational programmes, where the overall purpose of assessment is to determine whether a person is competent to work in a particular environment.

29 Creating learning archives

On many courses, students do a series of separate assignments on separate modules and so are implicitly discouraged from making comparisons between their assignments. They are in fact almost certainly learning and developing from one assignment to another but they will probably remain unaware of their progress unless it is pointed out to them. If you ask your students to start building up an archive of their assessed work and comparing their earlier efforts with their more recent achievements, this will reassure them about their progress and act as a motivator; students who have evidence of their progress are stimulated to achieve more. Archives can also be introduced as a more structured part of the curriculum. For example:

Archives in the classroom
Ask your second year students to bring in their first year essays. Run a session in which they re-read the essays, specify what they have learned since they completed them, and describe how they have progressed. They could do this in the round or in sub-groups, depending on numbers.

Ask the same question
If you set students an essay question in their first year and the same question again in their second or third year and ask them to compare the two, this will demonstrate to them how differently they write essays now. The best topics to use are those which lend themselves to treatment at various depths by students at different stages in their development. An example is the sociology essay question, 'What are some of the causes of juvenile crime?' This essay can be set at any stage from high school to postgraduate study. You can, of course, only use this method with students who have followed a similar course to each other; if you want to use it

on a modular course where students follow different routes, you will need to set questions that can be answered from different perspectives.

Show the same visual material

This method is similar to the previous one but covers a shorter time span. Show students some visual material, such as a piece of anthropology film, a piece of artwork, or a set of haematology slides, at the beginning of a module or section of a course and ask them to note down what they see. Show it to them again when they have learned how to look at material from an academic perspective and then get them to specify the progress that they have made. This method can be used in conjunction with many of the assessments in this book.

Use the same checklist

If you have an assessment checklist for your students, such as a set of objectives or criteria for marking, you can help them to monitor their progress by encouraging them to rate themselves regularly according to the checklist. For example, for some professional placements, there is a list of situations, skills, and/or behaviours in which a student should be competent. By regularly revisiting the same checklist, either alone or with a tutor, students can see what progress they are making and where they need more training or experience.

Chapter 8
Assessing group work

30 Shared group grade

In group project work, students generally work as teams to conduct a project, produce a report or other assessment, and then one mark is awarded to the group. Such a collaborative approach can produce high quality work, help students to develop the ability to work effectively with others, and can reduce marking load. However, despite these benefits, this type of assessment strategy can also give rise to a number of problems.

When single marks are given to a group, they are usually higher, on average, than those given to individual pieces of work. Groups can achieve more than individuals, and individual weaknesses tend to be covered up by the strengths of other group members. Group marks also often vary less than individual marks. If groups are randomly formed, the average ability of the members of the groups will be similar and will lead to a narrow overall spread of marks. On many courses it is unacceptable for marks to be uniformly high. However, if the assessment is sufficiently challenging, and the mark scheme robust, this can usually either be overcome or at least justified.

Harder to address are the issues surrounding the perceived 'fairness' of awarding a single group mark to all group members, regardless of their individual contributions. In this situation, it is possible for low contributors to be 'carried' by the high contributors without incurring a penalty.The difficulty of arriving at a fair mark for individuals is one of the most common reasons for not using group work for assessment purposes, despite its many advantages for learning.

Some courses cope with these problems by weighting the mark for the group project in such a way that it counts for only a small proportion of the individual student's overall result. This reduces student dissatisfaction and the perceived sense of unfairness, but can also undermine the importance of group work and reduce investment in the assessment. Another common approach is to attempt to recognise individual's contributions to the group work (see items **31** and **32**).

However, a less common strategy that may have considerable benefits is to educate students about working in groups, emphasising the process, rather than just the end product. With this approach, early sessions introduce the students to a variety of effective group management strategies and provide opportunities to try them out. For example, students can be asked to produce project plans, allocate roles, and develop agreements about expected contributions and the consequences of not complying. These should include discussion of distributing work efficiently, making plans to edit and revise one another's contributions, and determining how they will agree final versions. Participation in this stage could be informal, conducted as workshop-style activities, or could be more formally assessed using reflective diaries (see item **26**).

Focussing on the process, rather than just the end product, has a number of benefits. It increases the sense of communal ownership over the final report, and can therefore reduce dissatisfaction with the perceived fairness of group assessment. In the long term, this approach also helps students to develop a more collaborative approach, in which they neither under-contribute, nor over-dominate the workload. These are important employability skills, preparing students for working in teams effectively in the future. This aspect can be emphasised by using real-life scenarios in the tasks and by working with alumni or appropriate community partners.

31 Supervisor assessment of contribution

In group work, and in some extended pieces of individual work, the specific contribution of an individual to a piece of work isn't always clear. For example, in a group, students can be either 'carried', or, conversely, let down, by their peers' contribution to the piece of work. Even in individual work, such as dissertations, it can be difficult for an independent marker to determine how much support and guidance the student needed to complete the work. In these scenarios, supervisor assessment of an individual's contribution can be crucial, but must be carefully considered.

Supervisor's assessment of individual contribution to group work

In some situations, it may be possible for a supervisor to assign individual student marks for group work. For example, in presentations and exhibitions (see items **10** and **11**), they may ask each student to cover a different section of the task and/or to separately respond to questions. Although the group is likely to have helped each other prepare (and indeed should be encouraged to do so), it is usually possible to distinguish between the students that really understand the topic and who have committed time to the project, and those who are relying on the others. However, where the required work is more integrated, or where only a written piece of work is submitted, this may not be an effective means of distributing marks.

Alternatively, a mark could be awarded for the final piece of work, but also a separate mark for the supervisor's perception of the individual group members' contributions. In this situation, the mark given to the individual would focus on the process of group work (assessing 'conduct'), and then the group would receive an overall mark for the end product. This balances the need to produce a high quality, united piece of work from the group, with the necessity to also perform effectively as an individual. However, this does rely on the supervisor being able to observe the group process sufficiently to award an appropriate mark; this may be more appropriate in laboratory-style projects in which they are likely to spend more time with the students during the work. These marks could also be further informed by peer assessment of contributions (see item **32**).

Supervisor's assessment of a student's contribution to individual extended work

The contribution of a student to their dissertation or project can vary considerably and is not always apparent in the final piece of work. For example, they may have come up with the original idea themselves, negotiated access to novel resources, and/or submitted prompt and high quality drafts for comments. Alternatively, they may have needed considerable support to conceptualise and carry out the work, regular reminders about submitting work, and substantial amounts of detailed feedback. While it is possible to mark a piece of work 'on its own merits' without regard for this information, assessment criteria usually include such factors as the initiative taken by the student, the creativity of the student and so on. As most pieces of major work are now marked anonymously by more than one person, this sort of contextual information can be difficult to assess.

To get around such problems, the supervisor can complete a basic assessment of the student's contribution. For example, the checklist below includes rating scales for different components of the student's contribution; it can be completed relatively quickly, and is in a form that is easy to interpret and quantify if necessary. This can be used to either calculate a mark that forms a separate component from the written work itself, or could be passed to markers to be taken into account when awarding an overall mark.

Supervisor's sheet: assessment of student contribution

	Low/ Poor				High/ Excellent
1. Contribution to choice of topic	1	2	3	4	5
2. Theoretical contribution	1	2	3	4	5
3. Contribution to experimental design	1	2	3	4	5
4. Experimental technique	1	2	3	4	5
5. Data analysis and statistical treatment of results	1	2	3	4	5
6. Interpretation of results	1	2	3	4	5
7. Impression of student's grasp of topic	1	2	3	4	5
8. Workload involved in the topic	1	2	3	4	5

Additional remarks from supervisor

....

....

Signed ....

32 Student assessment of contribution

Although shared group grades and supervisor assessments can be useful approaches to assessing group work (see items **30** and **31**), the students themselves are often in the best position to assess individual contributions. This can either be done on an individual level or with group agreement. With appropriate guidance, this is a useful insight into the group process, and can encourage a reflective approach. It can even be used to guide behaviour during the group work process, by asking students to give each other indicative comments/marks at a midway stage as formative feedback, before giving the final summative mark on completion of the project.

Dividing marks between students

One approach is to give the group a number of marks, based on the quality of their end product, and allow them to divide this amongst themselves in a way which they think reflects the relative contributions of individuals. For example, if a group of five students were to be awarded 60 per cent for a group report, they would be given 5 x 60 = 300 marks to distribute among themselves.

Students may decide at the outset to simply divide marks equally. This is often seen to reduce potential conflict, but it risks some group members doing very little work and others becoming resentful. In contrast, other groups will not discuss assessment at all until it is time to divide up the marks. This can then cause difficulties, if they disagree about the basis upon which the marks should be allocated. However, if the allocation method is determined in advance, they will all be clear about what their contribution ought to be, and will be more likely to accept the final allocation of marks. Tutors can help with this process by organising discussion and negotiation of criteria at the start of the project. Alternatively, you can impose criteria of your own which the students then use to allocate the marks.

An important caveat to this approach is that it encourages individual students to 'take over' the project. The most marks are available for someone who the whole group agrees did all the work, rather than one who successfully encourages contributions from all members. The criteria should, therefore, include consideration of how to distribute marks between those who do too much as well as those who do too little.

Awarding marks for contribution

An alternative approach is to simply award marks to an individual according to their group's perception of their contribution. In this case, the best marks could go to all members of a team who contributed well and equally, rather than being awarded on the competitive basis outlined above. This can then be used as a multiplier for the awarded mark, or to contribute to a 'conduct' component of the module mark.

For example, in the rating sheet given below, students are required to rate all other members of their group in terms of several key aspects of their contribution to the group's work. As above, it is important to make these criteria clear at the outset. The average rating for each individual is then deducted from the group mark and that deducted score allocated to that individual as her or his mark. In this case a student who made a major contribution to the group's work in every respect would have an average rating of 0 and receive the group grade for the piece of work. A student who contributed little to the group's work in all of these respects would receive the group grade minus 12 marks. The criteria used here are for illustration only: other criteria concerning creativity, supportiveness in the group, or ability to keep to deadlines could equally be used. Alternatively, criteria could specify aspects of the project such as research, organisation of data, report writing, and presentation of findings. Similarly the weightings can be adjusted to reflect the most important aspects of contribution.

Peer assessment of contribution to group rating sheet

Student . . . .

has contributed to the group's work in the following ways:

	Major contribution	Some contribution	Little contribution
1. Leadership and direction	0	−1	−2
2. Organisation	0	−1	−2
3. Ideas and suggestions	0	−1	−2
4. Data collection	0	−1	−2
5. Data analysis	0	−1	−2
6. Report writing	0	−1	−2

Chapter 9
Examinations

33 Standard exam

University exams take a variety of formats but typically comprise a series of tasks, such as multiple choice or short answer questions, calculations, or essays, to be completed individually and within a particular time limit. They are, therefore, a test of the student's ability to recall key material under pressure. Depending on how they are structured, they also test their understanding of the material, and their ability to use it effectively, within the allotted time. Upcoming exams encourage students to focus, and read and learn more extensively than they would without this incentive.

A distinct advantage of the exam format is the controlled conditions. As long as there is appropriate invigilation and identity checking, it is one of the few assessment settings in which you can be confident that the student completed the work themselves. This is in contrast to many coursework-based assignments, where plagiarism and collusion remain a risk despite technological advances in detection (see item **52**).

In addition, exams can be marked anonymously, particularly as tutors are no longer likely to be familiar with their students' handwriting. This is an advantage over forms of assessment where this anonymity cannot be preserved (e.g. presentations, placements) and helps reduce bias based on gender, race, personality or other factors. However, as with any assessment, there remains the risk of bias towards answers putting forward arguments with which the author agrees; this may be a particular challenge in more discursive subjects and should be addressed in the marking criteria.

However, there are also disadvantages to the exam format. They may put students under undue pressure, and there is no guarantee that the work they produce on the day is their best possible performance. This may particularly discriminate against those who write more slowly, those who like to consider arguments for longer, those with poor or unpredictable health, and/or those who are prone to anxiety. Processes should be in place therefore to manage some of these difficulties, including support for students who are worried about exams and clear guidelines for what to do if they are ill on the day of the test (see item **51**).

By relying simply on recall, traditional exams also give limited opportunities to demonstrate what can be produced with access to appropriate resources, such as reference material. As such, some consider that they are not an accurate reflection of the student's ability to perform in 'real life'. However, there are multiple ways to adapt the exam format to address these concerns and maximise opportunities for all, as can be seen in the rest of this chapter.

34 Open book exam

An open book exam, in which students are permitted access to supporting materials, reduces the need for memorisation and instead focuses on their ability to use resources and their own understanding to answer questions. In practice, this is more similar to the 'real' world; professionals do not rely heavily on memory for information, instead keeping key textbooks and other reference sources at hand and consulting them when needed. They have to be familiar with these sources, but they probably do not need to memorise much of their contents. Indeed, the skills required for using resources quickly and effectively may themselves be worth assessing.

This is already standard practice in some subjects. For example, in many English literature exams, key texts can be brought in, because students are being tested on what they can say about the pieces, rather than what they can remember or quote from them. In other cases, engineering students may be given access to specific computer programs and online resources, so that problem solving in the exam more closely simulates the way working engineers operate. However, many other subjects could benefit from such an approach. It can encourage more understanding-focussed revision, as students do not have to be concerned with rote learning. Further, allowing students access to such sources enables staff to set more complex questions than in conventional exams.

A common objection to open book exams come from tutors who believe that students need to be tested on their memory for facts, definitions or algorithmic procedures, all of which are readily available in textbooks. If this is the main purpose of the test, then it is true that this style of exam is unlikely to be best practice. Instead, its utility is more appropriate to higher level exams where the assessment focuses on the ability to argue a case, to criticise evidence, or to demonstrate understanding and synthesis.

A more valid concern regards controlling the nature of the materials to which the student has access. If the permitted materials are paper based, then this is relatively straightforward, although it is important for invigilators to check the materials for unauthorised annotations. Giving access to computers and/or online materials can be more complex, as it can be difficult to prevent students using additional resources that are not allowed under the regulations. This requires careful consideration by the module organiser and the exam invigilators.

35 Restricted-choice exam

Most students revise selectively for their exams. Their estimate of how many topics to learn is based on the number of topics covered on the exam paper and the amount of choice they are given. So, for example, if the exam paper is of the standard type where students are asked to answer, for example, three questions out of eight, most will begin by cutting five topics out of their revision schedule. An exam pass on a course that is examined in this way is no guarantee of coverage of the course.

One way to ensure that students cover enough ground in their revision to satisfy you that they have engaged with the course is to adjust the number of questions and the extent of the choice in the exam. Other ways include setting an obligatory broad-based question or an obligatory section containing short questions on a large number of topics.

You can of course take this further and eliminate choice entirely, in which case your exam paper will have the rubric 'Answer all the questions'. This can be unpopular among students, but combines particularly well with a seen exam (see item **36**). In this way students are obliged to study as many of the topics as you include on the list of questions.

36 Seen exam

It can be argued that conventional three-hour unseen exams, with no access to books, notes or other resources, are a rather curious way of testing ability. Students will probably never face the same kind of test under such extreme time pressure in any subsequent work. Exams even bear little resemblance to independent postgraduate research. A more realistic way of testing students would assess their ability to research, use resources, draft and redraft.

Seen exams, in which students are given copies of the exam paper prior to the exam, test these abilities. They also eliminate the element of luck involved in question spotting. Students are less anxious about the exam and their answers are of a higher quality. This type of exam is often popular because it is seen to offer the advantages of both exams and coursework. There are two main types of seen exam. In both cases, the student sits a formal exam, but they have been given the questions at different periods in advance.

The nine-month exam

If you give students copies of the exam paper at the beginning of the course, this will act as a course map, indicating to them which parts of it are important and which are peripheral. The main problem with the nine-month exam is that students may orient themselves narrowly to the exam questions and take unexamined topics less seriously during the course. This can be minimised by setting broad and theoretical questions which have no right answers and which require considerable thought rather than mere reproduction. Another approach is to give a selection of questions at the beginning of the course, with the instruction that some (but not all) of these questions will be in the final exam, and that the students will be required to answer all questions. Students then need to ensure that they prepare for the full range of possible topics.

The one-week exam

This format consists of giving students copies of the exam paper one week before the exam date, during which time they can use their notes, the library and other resources. In a sense the one-week exam is simply an important end-of-course assignment with a one-week time limit. However, if the time allowed for writing the exam is kept short, it is likely to be shorter in length than an assignment and so less of a burden for the markers. The one-week exam does have some practical disadvantages; focusing on it can be disruptive of other courses or exams and it puts a lot of pressure on library provision, though this can be minimised by placing crucial books on very short loan.

A problem with either scenario is that students may memorise whole answers. The exam itself can then become an exercise in writing out from memory an answer prepared some time before. However, this may not matter much provided that the original learning and answer development has been undertaken. Another problem that is less easily addressed is that of collusion; as with any coursework, this style of exam leaves open the possibility that the student being assessed has not completed the work themselves. Although they would need to regurgitate the answer in the exam itself, there is no guarantee that they researched and planned it independently. This type of question may be best used in conjunction with other, non-seen questions to help address this issue. Alternatively, a short viva or presentation can be used in conjunction with a seen exam to verify understanding.

37 Project exam

There are occasions where the main learning activity on a course is some kind of practical or project work but where there is still some necessity for a formal written exam. This may be because external validating bodies or professional bodies require an exam, or it may be because the staff consider an exam to be desirable.

Conventional essay-based exams can distort the aims of the course by distracting students from their projects. Instead, project exams focus on more applied questions that are directly related to their project work. For example, students who undertake an industrial case study that is mainly assessed as a written report or portfolio, can then be asked in an exam about how they would respond to hypothetical situations.

Q. If there were a three-month national building strike starting on week 3 of your case study, how would this affect your handling of the case?

Q. If outline planning consent were granted for a competitor organisation on week 14 of your case study (see details below), how would you advise your client?

Students would have their log books and other case material to hand (see item **34**) and would be expected to use these in answering the questions. Such questions cannot be answered from memory, or even directly from this information, but only from students' experience and understanding of the case study.

This type of exam may be particularly useful where the case study is conducted as a group project. The exam is therefore designed to test individuals' understanding and to produce a mark for each individual student.

The exam questions can also require students to explain a particular theory, or to compare two competing theories, using examples from their own practical experiences. This form of exam has the added advantage that if students know at the outset that they will be expected to answer questions of this type, they are more likely to be reflective about theory and general principles during their experience. This keeps the students focussed and helps prevent them getting overwhelmed with practical details and forgetting the purpose of the exercise.

38 Adapting assessments for exam settings

Exam formats are usually selected from a relatively limited range of options. Items **33–37** outline some other options that could be considered, to extend the range of skills testing in an exam setting. However, many of the innovative assessments outlined in this book could also be adapted for use in exams. For example, students could be given a research question, and asked to design a simple experiment to test the hypothesis (see item **16**). Alternatively, they could be given text from a wiki on a particular topic, and asked to highlight key misunderstandings and inaccuracies, and to provide replacement text (see item **20**).

When adapting assessments for exam settings, it's important to consider how the limited time affects the task. If written materials are provided for analysis and response, they must be of an appropriate length; the assessment should not be about the speed of reading, but rather the ability to understand and critique appropriately.

Chapter 10
Involving students in the assessment process

39 Peer assessment

Involving students in marking can promote a genuine understanding of assessment, and the processes that underpin it. It gives students the opportunity to see and reflect on the work of others which, at least for written work, is quite rare. Peer assessment also helps develop the ability to discriminate between different pieces of work, and the criteria that define its quality. This clarifies student understanding, as it may be the first time that they have seen, for example, the effective synthesis of different theories or ideas. In doing so, it leads to students critically appraising their *own* work, understanding how it compares with others in the cohort, and recognising and addressing weak areas.

In spite of these benefits, tutors are often reluctant to introduce peer assessment in classes. This is typically due to fears that the final outcome(s) will be unreliable. This is a very real hazard since students: (i) are likely to be poorly informed on the topic; (ii) may be uncritical, or unable to differentiate quality; and (iii) may not be objective due to personal factors. In addition, the administration of a peer assessment system is also complex and time consuming; it is certainly not an easy way out of a marking load. However, many of the potential hazards can be reduced or avoided by following these principles.

Start early (and small)

Although students may have experience of peer assessment in school, they are likely to be concerned about the ability of undergraduates to assess university-level work, and therefore the potential for unreliability and/or unfairness. Therefore, it is a good idea to introduce the process in the first year, to develop their expertise and trust in the approach. This is also an opportunity to introduce them to peer assessment in the context of formative assessment, or where the peer-assessed mark is only a small component of the final grade.

Briefing the students

For students to feel confident and comfortable with their role as peer assessor, and as the recipient of peer assessment, they must be briefed well at the start of the process. Providing a detailed outline of the procedure, including time allocated for each stage, can reassure students and reduce the chance of any ambiguities. In addition though, it is also important to explain the rationale behind peer assessment and the intended learning outcomes.

Make it easy and clearly structured

Start with simple pieces of assessment with relatively objective marking criteria. For example, this could include marking graphs of data collected in a laboratory, where students have to check whether axes are labelled appropriately and so on. For more open assessments, such as short oral presentations, it is useful to provide detailed marking criteria, in which students are simply required to indicate their mark on a rating scale. Students often dislike giving negative feedback, so this can be facilitated asking them to select from a list of frequent and/or typical errors. This approach makes the results more consistent and reliable; a space for open comments then allows more detailed, supplementary feedback.

Use multiple anonymous markers

It is necessary to keep the assessors anonymous to avoid peer pressure and bias. In written work, ID numbers can be used instead of names to make this process 'double blind': the assessors do not know who they are marking and the students do not know who has marked them. In the case of presentations, it is clearly not possible for the identity of students to be kept anonymous, but it is possible to arrange matters so that students do not know who has marked them. Several markers should be used for each piece of work, and the marks should be returned in the form of an average mark. This also gives staff the opportunity to screen the comments given by assessors to ensure that they are appropriate and constructive. It is important to set up efficient systems to manage this process in advance, to minimise the administrative burden.

Review the process afterwards

Peer assessment is an engaging approach for many students. If the process goes well, with apparently reliable outcomes and sensible and/or constructive feedback, students should be suitably praised. Comparing peer-assessed and faculty-assigned marks for the same piece of work can be an interesting process, particularly as they often align well. This process can help students further understand the criteria and refine their ability to critically appraise their own work.

Karl Nightingale

40 Students set the assignment titles

Students generally spend far more time answering questions than asking them, which is a pity, given that formulating questions is an invaluable aid to learning. If students are given the opportunity to devise their own assignment titles, it can encourage them to relate to their course in a deeper and more challenging way. They are also likely to be more motivated and so be likely to produce better assignments if they are writing on topics that they have chosen themselves. There is a concern that students may avoid topics which are perceived as harder, or for which they feel they will get lower marks. It may, therefore, be necessary to set some boundaries about which topic areas need to be covered by the questions.

A variety of ways of achieving this is suggested here. The suggestions range from those where the tutor retains some control to those where the students have full independence. It is likely that different methods would be appropriate depending on the level and experience of the students and the weighting of the assessment.

Individual student

Here students have total freedom to do what they like. There are no restrictions on them but on the other hand they receive no support. This method encourages autonomy in students but means they may experience feelings of isolation. It also risks students identifying a topic that is not feasible or appropriate for the course, without the opportunity to be guided towards something more suitable.

Individual students with group feedback

Students are asked to devise their own titles, and then seek feedback from their seminar group. This can be with or without the tutor present. The benefits of this method are that students share their ideas and also receive individual feedback. With a group whose members have learned to trust one another, it works very well. It may be less effective if students are concerned about others copying their title ideas and so on.

Individual students with tutor

Students are asked to devise their own titles in consultation with their tutor. This gives them the opportunity to choose their own topic but with guidance from the tutor on the wording of the question. This is the method which requires most tutor time, but leads to a good balance of autonomy and support for the student. This approach is sometimes adopted with large assignments, where independent thought is important, such as a final year dissertation.

Individual students and student groups with tutor

Individual students are invited to submit suggestions for assignment titles. They then brainstorm their ideas as a group and select a variety for submission. The suggested titles are considered for inclusion on the assignment list by a panel of staff and students, before a shortlist of titles for students to choose from is agreed. The benefits of this method are that students share their ideas and the assignment list, being the work of many hands, is very rich.

41 Students negotiate the marking criteria

Assessment criteria are normally fixed by teaching staff. A useful alternative is for students to negotiate their own criteria with one another and with their tutor. This ensures not only that they know what the criteria are, but also that they understand why they have been selected and recognise their relevance. It also gives them the opportunity to make their own proposals about assessment. There are various ways in which students can be involved in negotiating the assessment criteria.

Unstructured discussion

If students have had experience of taking responsibility for their own learning, it may be enough just to say to them 'I suggest that you propose your own criteria for assessing the next assignment. I'll allow half an hour at the end of this session for you to discuss assessment and draw up a list of criteria.' You may like to stay and observe their discussion so that you understand the thinking behind their conclusions or you may feel that they will work better if you leave them on their own.

Structured discussion

If your students need a little more structure, you may wish to give prompts to stimulate ideas. For example, they could all note down individually the characteristics of 'the best essay I ever wrote' or could get into groups and note down the characteristics of 'the perfect essay'. Alternatively, the prompts could be more specific, and ask them to complete sentences such as 'I would like to be given credit for...' or 'I think people should be penalised for...'.

Inference

Another method is to start from criteria that are already in operation. For this each student brings a piece of work which has already been marked, and uses it to analyse the feedback they received. From this, they should infer what criteria have been used to mark it. From these notes, the group develops a coherent set of inferred criteria, and then discusses whether these criteria are satisfactory or whether they can improve on them. This has the added benefit of helping students to explore, and reflect on, their feedback in more detail (see item **46**).

Chaired discussion

If the students are not used to taking responsibility for their own learning, or have never had this type of responsibility before, they may need the tutor to chair the discussion, before they can agree on their criteria. After any method of devising the student-led criteria, the students must then negotiate with the tutor to finalise the mark scheme. Again, there are various ways of approaching this.

Accept the students' criteria

The tutor may decide to accept the students' criteria, as a matter of principle, from the start. This could be because their criteria are likely to be good and accepting them shows you have confidence in their capabilities. Alternatively, it could be because the criteria are likely to be flawed, but using them anyway could be a useful learning opportunity. This latter option is likely to only apply for formative pieces of coursework, where the stakes are not too high. It may be particularly appropriate where students are to produce a series of assignments and are encouraged to re-negotiate the criteria for each piece of work.

Challenge the students' criteria

To encourage students to see the flaws in their criteria, the tutor could play a challenging role and ask questions of the type 'What do you mean by ...?' or 'How do you justify...?' or 'Why did you include ...?' or 'What if ...?' The outcome of this method is an amended version of the students' criteria.

Show the students your own criteria

This is the method that leaves most control in the hands of the tutor. The students can be shown the tutor's criteria and asked to make comments, criticisms and suggestions based on their own discussions. The outcome of this method is an amended version of the tutor's criteria.

Whatever method is adopted, the process needs to start early so that students are clear on the mark scheme before they start their piece of work.

Chapter 11
Feedback to students

42 Giving effective feedback

Effective feedback helps students to understand the gap between their current performance and the level at which they would like, or are required, to perform. It also helps them consider how they can navigate this gap and attain a higher level of performance. Markers can spend considerable amounts of time writing extensive feedback, but if it is not focused appropriately, and/or it is not received and used effectively by the student, then it is unlikely to improve work in the future. This can lead to frustration for marker and student alike.

There are a variety of different ways in which effective feedback can be given, although written comments on submitted work remain the most common. This allows in-text annotations, and/or more generalised comments at the end of the piece of work. Other approaches, including pro formas and the use of audio-visual technology are discussed later in this chapter. Whatever mode of delivery is selected, there are a number of more general considerations to ensure that the feedback is effective and efficient.

Qualities of effective feedback

If feedback is to influence future behaviour, it must be clear, specific and solution focused. It is usually best to avoid using very short comments, symbols or other notation without explanations. Students are unlikely to be able to interpret what is meant by a question mark, exclamation mark, or single words in the margin. For example, rather than just noting that a section is 'unclear', it is more informative to explain to the student what makes the section unclear. This could be the use of excessively long sentences, changing topics rapidly without warning, or inaccurate use of technical terms. Offering a potential solution (e.g. 'Try to work systematically through each study in turn, rather than jumping between them') gives practical guidance for improvements on their next assessment. Similarly, if a piece of work has many errors in it, it is more useful to comment on how the student could avoid this, rather than just pointing out all the mistakes. This could include recommending that a student checks all key facts against the textbook before submission, contacts a member of staff if there are aspects that they are very unclear on, or leaves enough time to proofread their work thoroughly.

Feedback often works best when it is selective. It is easy to become overwhelmed by too many comments and students may be unable to pick apart which aspects are really important to improve and which are more minor comments. The marker can guide their attention by selecting two or three key points to emphasise, so that the student can focus their efforts. These selected aspects should be areas that would make the largest improvement to a student's attainment. As well as being more useful for the student, this selectivity can also be more efficient for the marker; instead of commenting on every area that could be improved, they can focus instead on their identified priorities. It is also important to ensure that the tone of the comments is, overall, matched to the grade given. It can be confusing to be given a relatively low mark if there are mainly positive comments throughout the manuscript. Similarly, a student can be disconcerted to receive a good mark for a script that is covered in negative comments, with few explanations of how they achieved the grade.

The most useful feedback is likely to cover both strengths and weaknesses of a piece of work, rather than just pointing out errors. This helps to build confidence in the student, but also enables them to understand what they are doing well so they can ensure they maintain this standard. In this way, positive comments should be just as specific as constructive criticism; if students are unclear what they are doing that warrants a comment of 'good', then they will be less likely to repeat it in the future. This also ensures that students of all abilities continue to improve their work. It is easy to provide only negative comments to weaker students, who may need a confidence boost more than most. Similarly, very able students may get frustrated if all their comments are positive and they are not guided by constructive criticism to help them improve their performance further.

The importance of feedback timeliness is often emphasised, and indeed measured, in higher education. There will usually be a deadline by which your institution expects feedback to be given to students. Timely feedback makes it more likely that a student will engage with, and learn from, the feedback. If the piece of work feels like a long time ago, then they are more likely to simply look at the mark and disregard the comments. However, the tutor must balance the advantages of providing quick feedback, which is often inevitably in less detail, with the benefits of more in-depth comments. The relative importance of speed versus depth is likely to vary depending on the nature of the piece of work. However, in any circumstance, the timing of the next piece of assessment should be considered, either in your own module or others on the course as a whole. If students are to use your comments in future work, in a 'feedforward' mechanism, then they must receive the comments on their previous piece of work prior to submission of the next. Highlighting the opportunities to do this can be a useful way of engaging students with their feedback (see item **46**).

Feedback can vary considerably between different markers. To help standardise provision, it may be useful to introduce a checklist of desired qualities to help guide the process. This could include questions such as 'Have you identified and explained a key strength and a key weakness of the piece of work?', 'Have you given at least one specific thing that the student could do in their next piece of work?', and/or 'Do your comments match the grade given?'. This needn't be a 'top-down' list imposed on the markers by leadership teams, but could instead be generated by the staff team as part of an exercise to enhance feedback.

43 Feedback pro formas

Giving high quality feedback is a time-consuming process, and tutors often find themselves writing the same comments numerous times on different students' work. For this reason, it has become relatively common to produce feedback pro forma sheets that markers complete instead of extensive annotations on the piece of work itself. If designed appropriately, these provide detailed comments for students in an efficient way. There are a number of different structures that can be adopted.

Checkbox sheet

This type of pro forma includes a number of feedback comments based on either required elements (e.g. 'Graph is missing a label on the axes' or 'References not in requested format') or on common strengths and weaknesses of student work ('Introduction includes a good explanation of the context and scope of the essay' or 'Good use of evidence to back up your point'). This list can be generated based on previous experiences of marking a particular assessment or, for new assessments, by pre-marking a subset of the work to see the common issues. It can also include more generic aspects, such as common errors of spelling and punctuation. Once the list is developed, the marker can then simply tick which comments apply to each piece of work, and return this to the student. If the list is numbered, markers can supplement this sheet by writing the number of the comment next to an example in the text. The checkbox sheet is one of the most efficient ways to give feedback but can be seen as impersonal by the students. It works most easily where there are clear, objective criteria, rather than more nuanced arguments. However, in these cases, students can be encouraged to engage with this sheet by, for example, identifying examples, from their own work, of each comment ticked by the marker.

Online solutions

Many online marking software packages include a bank of standard feedback comments, and also allow the marker to generate their own list of generic comments. These can then be 'dragged and dropped' onto the piece of work at relevant points, and mixed with more personalised comments that are added for each student. This can offer a personalised experience for the students, while minimising the repetition on the part of the marker. If there is no access to a software package like this, a simple workaround can be to store a list of common comments in a separate word processing document, and then cut and paste those that are relevant, either as annotations onto the student's piece of work or onto a separate feedback sheet.

Structured narratives

In this type of pro forma, markers write narrative comments, but are guided by a series of prompts instead of simply writing 'freestyle' remarks at the end of a piece of work. These pro formas often take the form of a simple table, with the prompts in the left-hand column and then open boxes for comments against each prompt on the right. The prompts could include different qualities that are being encouraged in the piece. These may be relatively general, such as 'Analysis and argument', 'Range of sources used', and/or 'Structure and writing style', or refer much more specifically to the particular piece of work. Structured narrative sheets can also be used to prompt the marker to give both an example of a positive aspect that a student should keep doing in future, and an area that could be improved. Alternatively, they may be more solution focussed, and simply ask the marker to identify the three things that they would like the student to focus on doing in their next piece of work. Whatever the format, these sheets help ensure that staff cover all the different aspects of feedback in an efficient way.

Showing the students these forms in advance can also help them to develop their self-assessment skills (see items **39** and **47**).

44 Feedback on MCQs and short answer questions

It is time consuming to give feedback on short answer questions and MCQs, due to the large number of questions. In addition, as the same bank of questions is often used year to year, many tutors are concerned that the answers will 'leak' into the public domain, passed down between generations of students. This is, of course, frustrating, as good questions are difficult to write. However, it's important for students to receive feedback and to understand where they went wrong. There are several effective strategies, that are easily implemented without losing the integrity of the question bank, and which are extremely useful for student learning.

General tips

As always, there is a trade-off between the effort required from the marker, and how personalised the feedback is for individual students. It should be remembered that detailed feedback is most useful to students during the course, rather than on the final exam, so that they can use the feedback for improvement in the remainder of the course. Feedback should provide constructive and positive phrasings, pointing to resources where they can reinforce their knowledge. If they are well thought through, websites or specific page references in a book can help immensely. Generic statements such as 'refer to the textbook' with no further guidance should be avoided.

Generic whole-class feedback

A single document or lecture, summarising the class performance in an exam, can provide generic feedback. This should ideally cover each question in turn, or a selection of the most frequently failed questions, and should summarise common misunderstandings, and what the correct responses should have been. This is particularly straightforward for MCQ tests that have been scanned automatically, as the statistics for each question (e.g. percentage correct) can easily be generated. This is potentially the easiest mechanism for feedback in a very large class; it is low effort for the marker, but consequently less personalised for each student.

Pre-determined feedback per question

In many instances the tutor can anticipate the potential wrong answers to the MCQs and short answer questions they set. In this case, a short feedback paragraph for each potential wrong answer can be prepared in advance. All explanations can be distributed to all students, or these explanations can be compiled in a customised document for each student. If the test is carried out online, then the process can be set up to run automatically.

Peer feedback

Sometimes the best person to give feedback to a student is one of their fellow students. This is often less intimidating, and may provide perspectives that the tutor had never considered. This can be done in a large group setting, in which each question is displayed in turn on the projector. For each question, the students are asked to write down what their answer would be, before then attempting to convince their neighbour that they have the right answer. The ensuing discussion often results in interesting debates, in which students are more willing to defend and argue their position than if the tutor disagreed with them. Finally, the tutor can reveal the correct answer. An optional add-on to this procedure is to use a classroom response system, or 'clickers' – small electronic devices that allow people to answer questions anonymously – to allow students to vote on the answer, and see the responses of others (see item **47**).

Live checking

In situations where there is a limited bank of questions, and it is desirable to protect the answers for future years, 'live checking' can be useful. Here students are asked to attend seminars where they can retrieve their exam paper and compare the answers they gave with answers and feedback that have been printed and displayed on a noticeboard. Students can check these under supervision of a staff member, and ask for clarification where appropriate. Students are not allowed to take away copies of their exam papers or the answers. It is important to remind students that they are not allowed to take photographs of the answers either. This process encourages students to engage with their answers and the correct answers, and to work out where their misunderstandings occurred.

Gavin Brown

45 Audio-visual feedback

Developments in technology have made it easier to give audio or audio-visual feedback to students. With audio feedback, markers record a verbal commentary on the assessment, either 'live' as they read it, or as a summary afterwards. Audio-visual feedback is similar, but the recording also includes the screen and allows the marker to point out specific parts of the work to which they are referring. This approach has been found to be generally popular among students, and allows a more informal, personal approach to feedback. When oral advice is recorded, rather than given in a face-to-face meeting, students can access it whenever they like, and listen to it multiple times if necessary. Giving feedback orally also allows tone and emphasis to make the meaning clearer; sometimes these nuances are lost in written comments, especially when written in haste, which can lead to either a point not being made strongly enough or to it being more upsetting than intended. In addition, the marker can often make more detailed comments in less time than the equivalent written feedback would take to compose.

Methods of giving audio-visual feedback

There are a variety of ways to give audio-visual feedback. At its most basic, it can be a Dictaphone recording, completed while reading the assessment either on paper or online. Alternatively, many mainstream software packages (e.g. Microsoft Word, Adobe Acrobat) now enable you to record audio comments and store them within the document itself. This gives the advantage of being able to link the comment to a particular section of text. In both cases, the recording or the audio-annotated document can be saved and sent to the student. Many virtual learning environments can also extend and automate this process. Here the marker views the submitted document online, records their comments either as audio or audio-visual recordings, and then uploads them to the university's virtual learning environment (VLE). In this case, there is no need to forward the files on to the student, as they are able to log in and view the comments when you put them online.

Technical issues

This form of feedback does have potential technical difficulties, although they tend to be easy to overcome. It relies on both marker and student having access to computers with recording and/or playback facilities; this is unlikely to be problematic for many. More of a problem may be the dissemination of the files. As they are often quite large files, there may be difficulties with emailing them, although this is avoided if a VLE is used. As with any form of feedback to students, it is important to keep a record: files should be labelled appropriately and stored securely.

Feedback prior to revisions

As well as feedback on submitted work, it is common to provide feedback on early drafts for later submission, particularly with more senior or postgraduate students. In this case, students are likely to want to be able to work their way systematically through the comments, and may not find a single narrative as useful as in-text comments. Short bursts of audio commentary, targeted at particular sections of the assessment, may be more appropriate here. More detailed textual suggestions, such as changes to punctuation or spelling, are likely to be better conveyed as additional written annotations.

46 Helping students to use feedback

One of the paradoxes of feedback is that markers often feel like they are spending a great deal of time providing comments and help, but students still feel that they are not receiving sufficient feedback to help them improve their performance. As well as increasing the quality of this feedback (see item **42**), it can also be useful to support students to use their feedback more effectively.

Student requests for feedback

One way of ensuring that students pay more attention to your feedback, and feel that it answers their needs directly, is to ask them what kind of feedback they want. This can be elicited from individuals or from the group as a whole. For example, the marker can ask the student to add a note at the end of the assignment, specifying what kind of feedback they would like. For example, they may have specific concerns about whether they have answered the question or included the appropriate level of detail. Alternatively, they may want you to refrain from commenting on punctuation or grammar and to focus instead on their demonstration of understanding. The students will probably need some encouragement the first time and an explanation of why you think it is a good idea, and maybe some examples of the kind of requests they might make.

If you want a request from the whole group, you can organise a discussion in which they address what type of feedback they find more and less useful, and come up with a list of general guidelines that the marker then uses. It is likely that they will state that the type of feedback they want depends on the nature of the assessment, so this may need to be repeated for each piece of work. If students are asked what kind of feedback they want, not only are they more likely to receive it, but they are more likely to be able to use it. An additional benefit is that their requests often constitute feedback to the tutor on her or his usual methods. For example, a student may say: 'Please try to give me constructive criticism and not just praise' or 'Please try to find a kinder way of telling me when I misunderstand things.'

Feedback exercises

When narrative feedback and marks are released at the same time, it is common for students to look at the mark and then only read the feedback in detail if they are unhappy with their performance. This is unfortunate, as the comments should help the students to improve in the future, even if they are already performing at a relatively adequate level. One way to improve engagement is to provide the narrative feedback a few days before the numerical marks are released. This encourages students to read the feedback, and they are likely to try to predict their grade based on these comments. Indeed, this can be built into a formal exercise, in which students predict their mark and then compare it to their actually awarded grade. You may even choose to withhold the numerical mark until the students submit a prediction of their grade and a brief commentary on their reasons. They can then be encouraged to talk with the marker if they had predicted substantially higher or lower, to ensure that they understand why they got that grade.

Feedforward sheets

Another approach specifically addresses feedforward, in which students use the comments that they receive on one piece of work to improve their performance on the next. Students can be asked to submit a brief form with their next piece of coursework, on which they have summarised the comments that they received in their last few assignments, and how they have addressed them in the current piece of work. By making this compulsory, it ensures that students revisit their past work, and consider the feedback for the new piece. In addition, it guides the marker to give feedback on the extent to which they have succeeded in addressing these issues. This is particularly useful with anonymous marking, where it is usually not possible to give follow-up feedback as the marker has no way of connecting the work to the previous submissions. A more extensive version of this is discussed in item **29**.

47 Self-assessment

One of the biggest challenges for a student is to know whether they are keeping up with the rest of the class, or falling behind. If the tutor takes responsibility for this, they must provide regular, well-structured and individualised feedback. Where classes are large, this can be challenging. Alternatively, the student can take responsibility, facilitated by the tutor providing 'self-assessment' questions.

Self-assessment questions are a type of formative question or exercise, which will not form part of the final grade, but from which the student will still get some quantitative appreciation of their performance. What distinguishes them from other types of formative assessment is the 'self' in self-assessment – the tutor is not involved in calculating a grade. This means that the assessment can be completed at times that are convenient for the student, repeated as often as needed, and feedback is immediate. In this way, students take responsibility for their own learning and monitoring their own performance. There are several different formats that these assessments could take.

Setting traditional 'homework' questions

A very common scheme is for the tutor to hand out the (non-assessed) questions, requiring the students to complete these as 'homework'. The model answers are then distributed the following week. Students then read the model answers, and resolve by themselves why their answers may not match up to the model ones. Providing some extra explanations with these model answers can help students understand common mistakes and how to resolve them. This approach encourages students to work independently, and to engage with the mark scheme, which can help understanding of future assessments (see items **41** and **49**).

However, if it is not clear why the answer is what you said, you may find that students need further input from you to understand where they went wrong. As the students complete these tasks offline, you will not get to see the class progress, as you will not have access to the marks. This can cause you to miss opportunities to help troubled students and/or to tailor the pace of your teaching sessions to personalise for the cohort.

Using peer feedback

In this scenario, a task is completed in class individually, under exam conditions. When everyone is finished, the tutor can go through the task, encouraging students to discuss their answers with their peers. At each stage, a volunteer can be asked to provide their answer or section of their answer to the whole class – students are far more likely to volunteer an answer if they have had opportunity to confer. If incorrect, care should be taken not to embarrass the volunteer. If correct, an explanation of why it is the right answer can be given by the tutor or another student. In this scenario, a student receives a suggested explanation from a fellow student and gets an authoritative answer from the tutor, which is an excellent combination for learning.

A further enhancement to this can be to use in-class 'clickers' (see item **44**). If the distribution of how the whole class answered is displayed (both before and after the 'peer discussion' stage), it enables all students to see how they are doing relative to everybody else. It also enables the tutor to see if there are any major misunderstandings, indicated by a large majority of the class going for the wrong answer. The anonymity aspect of this can also be a major advantage over simply raising hands. Students are all required to answer, and will feel more comfortable about making mistakes if these aren't visible to others. Unless the tutor uses individually registered handsets, they will not find out individual performance, but instead will get a general feel for the group's understanding. However, this requires significant use of class time, and can overrun if not managed correctly. This method also requires the tutor to think very quickly, responding to the class dynamic when there are misunderstandings; this ability develops with practice.

Automated feedback via online quizzes

If you have access to the appropriate technology, regular online quizzes can be useful (see items **5** and **6**). This can usually be conducted on university VLEs, or through independent free web-based software. Here the answers are revealed at the end of the quiz, or at a later date. The questions can take various forms including: true/false, multiple choice (MCQ), fill in the blanks, numeric or short answers. This strategy relies on the tutor to prepare good model answers, and good feedback text that anticipates wrong answers. However, an alternative or supplementary approach is to ask the students to create their own MCQs and then attempt and mark one another's answers (see item **22**). There are various pieces of software that allow this; some also create league tables of the best performances, the most popular questions, the most questions completed and so on.

A major advantage of online quizzes for the tutor is that you will likely have access to class statistics, observing how well the cohort or even individuals have done each week. This may allow you to adjust the pace of your teaching accordingly. For the students, they are able to repeat variants of the same quiz many times to practise and, in addition, can complete the work at their own pace without feeling pressured by exam conditions. A significant disadvantage of relying on online quizzes is the limitation of current technology – it is often quite difficult to automatically assess the answers if the model answer is a diagram or drawing, since current software is limited to short text answers or MCQs.

Motivating students to complete self-assessment questions

As self-assessment questions have no formal grade attached, it can be sometimes difficult to motivate students to complete these. There are different ways to address this issue. From a pragmatic perspective, a small amount of credit could be attached to the completion of these tasks. This would not be based on the performance, but merely on completion of the task. Alternatively, more intrinsic motivation can be encouraged by making it clear how these self-assessments relate to the summative assessments, and by making them an interesting and engaging part of the course. Where possible, you should keep track of the rates of participation and use these to encourage the students; there is evidence that people are more likely to comply if they are told that 'most of their peers' are completing the tasks, rather than focusing on the proportion of students that are not.

Gavin Brown

Chapter 12
Other considerations

48 Assuring assessment quality

At universities, the tutor who teaches a module is often also responsible for setting and marking the assessments. This often allows considerable freedom to tailor the curriculum to the areas of specialism and interest of staff and students, and to design engaging assessment tasks. However, this freedom also comes with much responsibility for the clarity, accuracy and appropriateness of the assessments, and the fair marking of the submissions. There are several processes that can be put in place to assure this process, including assessment scrutiny committees, moderators, and external examiners. Although the specific responsibilities may vary between institutions, the main tasks are during the design of the assessment, and then after the students submit their work.

Before the assessment is set: assessment scrutiny

Either an independent member of staff, or the appropriate committees, can check assessments and their mark schemes before they are given to students. With final year work, it is common for external examiners to also be involved in this process. Important factors to check include:

- the appropriateness of the assessment for the level of student (including adherence to any relevant university policies);
- the alignment between the assessment and the learning outcomes;
- the scope of the assessment (e.g. Is it realistic in the given timeframe?);
- the clarity of the task and its instructions;
- the accuracy and accessibility of the language used (e.g. Does it include culturally specific references that make it less inclusive?);
- the appropriateness of the mark weightings given to different sections;

- the accuracy and clarity of the mark scheme;
- whether any alternative correct answers should also be included in the mark scheme.

Following this consideration, the tutor who created the assessment and mark scheme will then have the opportunity to revise their materials before releasing them to students.

After submission of assessment: moderation

After the students have submitted their work, and marking commences, an internal moderator will usually assist in the assurance of this process. Depending on the level of the student and the weighting of the piece of work, this could include a variety of levels of involvement. For example, for small assignments and/or work in the earlier years, the moderator is likely just to review a sample of scripts and either confirm their agreement or discuss any issues with the tutor. For the most substantial pieces of work, such as dissertations, it is likely that there will be a system of blind double marking, in which two or more members of staff mark the (anonymised) work independently and then either average their marks or discuss their views and agree a final mark. Whatever level of moderation occurs, it is important to record the comments of the moderator and how any marks were agreed upon for future reference. This process should happen before the marks are released to students. In contrast, external examiners typically see the assessments after the end of the academic year, before the marks are formally approved by the board of examiners. Their role varies between institutions and anyone taking on this role should receive detailed training and guidance on local policies.

49 Mark schemes and criteria

Providing clear, explicit and appropriate mark schemes and criteria is a key component of successful assessment. It enables students to fully understand what they are expected to do and the standards by which their work will be judged. This is important because these standards can vary greatly according to the nature of the task, the subject, or the individual tutor who is marking the assessment. For example, some assessments may be designed to seek clear, concise and accurate summaries of a topic, whereas others may prioritise individual perspectives and opinions. Similarly, some parts of assessment may carry considerably more weight than others. Without clear mark schemes and/or criteria, it is impossible for the student to predict the requirements of any particular piece of work.

Explicit marking criteria also guide the behaviour, and therefore the learning, of the students. In the examples above, a student may spend more time on memorising key facts if they know accurate summaries are required, whereas they may emphasise wider reading and engaging in discussions with peers if they are clear that they need to develop and express their opinions on a topic.

Quality assurance

When many different markers are involved in assessing answers to the same questions, clear mark schemes and criteria can help standardise the grading. In this case, the mark schemes specify particular items that should be included in the assessment. Students accumulate marks according to how many of these specified 'targets' they manage to hit and how effectively they do so. Although the aim of such marking schemes is to increase consistency, they have some limitations. Firstly, they rarely differentiate 'key' points that should be made from more peripheral details. In this way, several marks could be gained by unstructured collections of accurate but poorly explained statements. It is useful to award more marks for more important points, or to allow scope for deductions if there are many details without a clear demonstration of overall understanding. Similarly, highly structured mark schemes can limit the extent to which innovation or original ideas are rewarded. It is important to build a degree of flexibility into the mark scheme to enable such recognition, particularly for higher level work.

Hidden criteria

Hidden criteria are those assessment criteria which affect students' grades but which are often not made explicit. These may include spelling, grammar, colloquial language, badly labelled diagrams, failure to state units of measurement and so on. Tutors may admit to their colleagues that such factors bias their response to the rest of the students' work, but they may not correct them or even comment on them consistently to the students themselves. Even if they do give feedback on these issues, the students may not realise the indirect effect they have on marks. It is useful to have open discussions with your students about your views on these 'hidden' criteria, so that they understand all factors that influence their grade.

Engaging students with marking criteria

Even when marking criteria are explicitly provided, students are not necessarily able to recognise and use this information. You can encourage students to engage more with the marking criteria by providing opportunities to try out using them on examples of previously submitted coursework, or by building some self-assessment into the process. As students become more familiar with the criteria, they will be better able to recognise how to develop their own work to meet these requirements (see items **39**, **41**, and **47**).

50 Staff marking exercise

If you were to ask a team of tutors for their criteria for assessment, it is likely that their responses would be largely consistent, although probably rather general. Such generalisations can mask real differences in expectations and priorities when marking assessments. One way of identifying and addressing any inconsistencies is to run a staff marking exercise. In such an exercise, tutors get together with copies of student assignments on the same topic, mark them, and compare their marks and comments. This then leads to a general discussion about assessment. The purpose of the exercise is not to mark the students, but to provide a forum in which tutors can discover how they compare with one another. In particular it clarifies the criteria that are being used in assessment.

This practice is common in courses with a large element of team marking, but it is equally important where staff are responsible for different assessments. As long as the chosen assessments are non-specialist enough to allow a variety of staff to be involved, it is possible to see very quickly whether they are adopting different standards and marking more strictly or more generously than their colleagues. It may also highlight differences in priorities. For example, tutors often put a different value on the dutiful, painstaking but dull piece of work and the quirky, unstructured witty piece. It is easy to include these elements in a list of criteria, but harder to be explicit about their relative importance. Staff marking exercises give an opportunity to explore these issues.

The following points are offered as guidance for running a marking exercise:

- Choose real examples of student work as a basis for discussion. Abstract discussions are much less fruitful. Even one example is very much better than none. Three or four examples are usually plenty: more can cause confusion and introduce more complexity and variation than staff can handle.

- Choose examples of moderate quality or perhaps of uneven quality with both good and bad features. It is relatively easy to agree on what is outstanding or awful, and little is learned through such easy agreements.
- Get staff to mark the examples all at the same time, during the exercise. If they do the marking too far in advance, there is a danger that they will either have forgotten details or formed a fixed and limited impression, perhaps with the expectation of having to defend it in public.
- Do not expect staff to make public their marks or opinions of the examples immediately. Allow them the opportunity to compare these with one or two others 'in private' first. This will make it much more likely that they will be flexible and receptive to the reality of differing values and perceptions which will inevitably be revealed.
- An attempt should be made to extract and discuss broad differences of principle underlying the variation in marks even if this proves difficult, rather than to go straight into seeking compromise and consensus on marks. There is unlikely to be any long-term effect on consistency unless the broad issues are tackled.
- Outcomes of the exercise should be clearly recorded, so that staff are supported to make sustained change, rather than slip back into old practices.
- Students should be informed of issues that have been resolved concerning criteria and standards.

51 Equal opportunities

Most universities express their commitment to equal opportunities for all students. In the UK, for example, institutional policies align with the Equality Act 2010. This names nine 'protected characteristics' that apply to education and training providers, employers and service providers: age; disability; gender reassignment; marriage or civil partnership (in employment only); pregnancy and maternity; race; religion or belief; sex; and sexual orientation.

Inclusive assessments, and assessment processes, are a key part of this commitment to equality. Although this can be a complex area to define, it is generally accepted that universities should offer all students equal opportunity to learn and participate, while maintaining academic standards. An effective starting point is providing a variety of modes of assessment. This makes it less likely that any individual or group of individuals will be consistently discriminated against, as different strengths and styles will be valued. Once this variety is established, there are a number of other strategies to enhance equal opportunities, including removing unnecessary or arbitrary barriers in assessments, reducing conscious and unconscious bias, and embracing and valuing diversity.

Removing barriers

There are a variety of ways in which barriers to participation in assessments can be removed. For example, in the case of students with disabilities, universities are required to make reasonable adjustments which could include altering the format of the assessment, giving extra time in exams, providing a scribe or reader, and producing materials in larger type or on coloured paper. Other adjustments such as allowing rest breaks in exams can also help students with other health conditions or extenuating circumstances. Similarly, it is advisable to allow students with religious beliefs to identify their rest days, holy days and festivals, and therefore, where possible, to avoid scheduling exams during these times.

A useful principle here is to focus on helping the student to remove the barrier early on, so that they have the opportunity to reach the same standard of performance as other students, rather than simply 'making allowances' after submission of the work. For example, for students with dyslexia, this could include providing regular learning support to help them to check their work for spelling or structural issues prior to submission, rather than identifying the work for sympathetic marking. Similarly, for students who suffer from anxiety during presentations, it may be beneficial to provide support and training to help them to overcome these difficulties. This could include anxiety management techniques, extra opportunities to rehearse, and the allowance to perform the presentation alone with the marker rather than with an audience of peers. Although more time intensive in the short term, this may be a better long-term solution than replacing all presentations with alternative assessments immediately.

Effective systems to monitor all these factors and the agreed resolutions are crucial, to ensure that all members of staff are aware of their responsibilities and can adhere to them consistently. This includes long-term conditions such as disabilities, but also more transient extenuating or mitigating circumstances. Both staff and students need to be aware of the processes by which extensions or other adjustments can be made in these situations.

Conscious and unconscious bias

Bias can occur when people consciously or unconsciously make assumptions about individuals based on identifiable characteristics such as those outlined above. Unconscious bias is particularly difficult to address because most people will not be aware of how this influences their attitudes and behaviour. Anonymous marking can be used in many situations to address this successfully. However, this is not appropriate in, for example, presentations, placements, or vivas. In these cases, common precautions can help minimise its impact. These could include recording presentations so they can be moderated, or having double marking in vivas. The most effective strategy, though, is education; training can raise awareness of these issues with members of staff, so that they can question the basis of their own judgements and those of others, and consider how they might be influenced by their own unconscious bias.

Embracing and valuing diversity

Embracing and valuing diversity starts from an inclusive curriculum, which covers a range of topics using examples from different cultures wherever possible. This can then be reflected in the assessments, through the choice of topics assessed, the assessment structure, or the language used. For example, questions should use gender neutral language, and mark schemes should give credit for examples from a variety of cultural backgrounds. This helps to ensure that all individuals, or groups of individuals, feel recognised and valued within the assessment structure.

52 Academic misconduct

Academic misconduct includes plagiarism, in which a student takes the work of others and passes it off as their own, and collusion, in which students work together in ways that are not permitted in order to deceive examiners. It can also include cheating in exams, through the use of unauthorised materials or other violations of the rules, and research misconduct such as fabricating data or the lack of observance of ethical principles. Helping students to avoid misconduct, as well as detecting and penalising offences, are important considerations for anyone involved in assessing students.

The first step is to understand why students commit academic misconduct. One of the most common explanations given is that the student felt under huge pressure, for a variety of reasons, and that plagiarism or cheating was their only option. Staff can help avoid this by checking assessment schedules for pressure points, and spreading out the submission dates or exams wherever possible. Sources of support for students with difficulties should also be made very clear and accessible, so that they realise that there are other ways to deal with their situation.

Education

Many instances of misconduct arise from misunderstandings either of what constitutes misconduct or a lack of appreciation of the seriousness of such behaviour. Therefore, it is good practice to provide information about all forms of misconduct, and its consequences, early in a student's academic career. This is particularly true of plagiarism, which students often struggle to understand fully. The opportunity to see examples of plagiarised work, and consider what is acceptable and what is not, can help to clarify matters. In this circumstance, plagiarism software is a useful training aid, as well as a detection device; students can benefit from seeing an annotated report and discussing the boundaries of acceptability. It can also be useful to discuss strategies for avoiding plagiarism, including note-taking strategies and referencing techniques.

Similarly, guidance should be given about good research practice, including how to keep effective records of primary sources or experiments, to help avoid other types of research misconduct. Overall, staff should be mindful that students from different cultures may have different understandings of appropriate behaviour. While being understanding of the legitimacy of their potentially differing beliefs, it is important that staff emphasise the need to adhere to their own university guidelines.

Assessment design

It is possible to design assessments to help make plagiarism and collusion less likely. For example, reflective pieces and portfolios require more individual input and make it harder to copy sections from other sources. Similarly, varying the assessments from year to year prevents collusion by students borrowing the work of senior students. With larger pieces of work, it is useful to give an opportunity for formative feedback, where a member of staff can highlight any areas of suspected plagiarism prior to formal submission. However, it's important to note that without putting the work through appropriate software, they may not spot all issues, and this can give students a false sense of security.

Administrative processes

As academic misconduct can have severe consequences for a student, including dismissal from the university, it is important to have transparent administrative processes in place. At the outset, students should be asked to complete training about academic misconduct and then sign a statement that they understand what it is and how to avoid it. This can encourage students to take responsibility for their own behaviour. While this can be a useful audit trail, it is clearly only meaningful if it is accompanied by genuine opportunities for students to ask questions and refine their understanding.

As plagiarism detection software improves, it is also increasingly important to have a clear policy for how it is used and interpreted. It is rarely an exact science, and the reports need the interpretation of a specialist in the academic field. As with students, staff benefit from the opportunity to see reports from this software and discuss what they believe is appropriate or not; this can help provide consistency in how plagiarism is treated.

Once any misconduct has been detected, there need to be clear guidelines in place for the chain of events that is now triggered. This is likely to be set at university level, and should include how a suspected student is contacted, what information they are given, and what right of response and representation they have. Following this closely is crucial to ensure just outcomes for the student and university alike.

53 Transcripts

The outcome of most assessment systems is a single grade or mark that is supposed to indicate the student's overall ability or achievement. This grade or mark may have been arrived at through the assessment of many distinct areas of knowledge and skills, and can be difficult to interpret by an outsider (or even, in many cases, by students or their tutors). For example, marks awarded are often norm-referenced, in which the assessment indicates how good one person is in relation to the total group being assessed. Even where there is not an explicit policy to mark on a curve, with set proportions of students getting each grade, the reality is that student performances are judged, to some extent, against each other. If an employer is not familiar with the general standard of students at a particular university, and the material that is covered in the course, then it hard for them to know what graduates with different grades are able to do. Further, a mark for a module may have been determined on the basis of a few different types of assessment, and it is typically impossible to decipher from the transcript whether a student is skilled at giving presentations, but less good at calculations, or whether they excel at writing in exam conditions but struggle on placements. While the format of formal transcripts is usually determined at university level, there may be supplementary material that could help students to display their skills appropriately.

Criterion-referenced assessments

Criterion-referenced assessments measure how an individual has performed on a task, quite independently of how others have performed. The outcomes of these assessments can then be presented as a list of demonstrated competencies. These are more common in vocational courses, targeted at particular professions, where there are clear expectations of performance. Criterion-referenced assessments can also help students to identify the acceptable learning outcome and whether or not further study is necessary. They can also encourage students to seek out opportunities to demonstrate specific competencies; this is useful on placements where opportunities to participate in different tasks and activities may vary (see item **28**).

Profiles

Even in traditional subjects, marks awarded could be presented in order to highlight specific areas of specialism or key skills. For example, by classifying each piece of assessment according to criteria, the marks can then be clustered to illustrate areas of strength. For example, in a Sport and Exercise Sciences degree, students may wish to demonstrate that they have strengths in some specific areas, such as sport psychology or exercise biochemistry, by giving an average mark for the groups of modules in each of the different disciplines. Alternatively, they may wish to display their ability to work in groups, or give oral presentations, and so could cluster assessments by format rather than topic. This sort of information is rarely offered to students, but could be a useful approach to displaying competence to prospective employers.